ESSEX'S OWN

DEE GORDON

T0346979

The
History
Press

First published 2009

The History Press
The Mill, Brimscombe Port
Stroud, Gloucestershire, GL5 2QG
www.thehistorypress.co.uk

British Library Cataloguing in Publication Data.
A catalogue record for this book is available from the British Library.

ISBN 978 0 7509 5121 0
Typesetting and origination by The History Press
Printed in Great Britain

Contents

Introduction

While delighted to be able to write about so many fascinating people from Essex, my brief of people 'from' Essex has meant that many associated with Essex have in fact been excluded. The focus, therefore, is on people born and/or brought up in Essex.

There are many people such as Dorothy L. Sayers and Joan Hickson (*Miss Marple*) who settled in Essex for many decades in later life. Similarly, there are others who came to Essex while still quite young (for example Lawrence Oates, the explorer), but after their formative years. Others, while 'from' Essex in the sense that they were born here have been excluded because they left the county, seemingly for good, within a couple of months or years – such as Jilly Cooper and Rik Mayall.

While some lesser-known individuals are included, there are many once-famous people, such as Sabine Baring-Gould (the writer), excluded: enough to fill another book – Forgotten Essex Folk perhaps. I have also had to limit the number of athletes, singers, writers, footballers and *EastEnders* actors as there are enough of these from Essex alone to fill yet another couple of books. The only Essex villain is Dick Turpin, because more recent transgressors are a) less well known and b) documented elsewhere. If a couple of people on your own Essex list are in fact missing, it is far more likely to be because of a lack of space than because of a lack of awareness of their existence. Choosing entries for such a book is also bound to have an element of subjectivity, for which, as the author, I make no apologies.

What remains is an eclectic collection to give readers, from Essex or elsewhere, just a taster of the range of people and talent produced here in Essex. Their impact on the history and culture of the county is significant not just at local level, but nationally and often internationally. If you find a few surprises here – people you didn't know were from Essex – all the better!

Dee Gordon

Acknowledgements

My husband and friends such as Donna Lowe, Pat Stone, Kim Kimber, Judith Williams, Debbi Hull and Debbi Campagna have had to put up with my ongoing 'what about him, what about her' regarding which people to include and exclude. Staff at Southend Library, particularly Simon Wallace, Sandra Cavalier and Susan Gough have been, as always, encouraging and enthusiastic, and the Essex Record Office and Answers Direct service have proved invaluable. In addition, libraries across the county (especially Redbridge, Billericay, Basildon and Frinton) have provided invaluable leads and snippets of information that I have been able to incorporate. A big thank you to them all.

The frustrating and time-consuming hunt for photographs has been alleviated by people I have literally stumbled across during researches. A special thank you to April and Sandra Phillips from Dagenham at: http://fun-autographs.tripod.com, who not only came up with some photographs, but also had useful tips on how to get hold of others (they are also committed fund-raisers via their charity website: www.bmycharity.com). There is, sadly, a very, very long list of celebrities, agents, photographers and webmasters who ignored my repeated letters and e-mails! Where efforts to trace copyright holders of photographs have failed, the publishers will be pleased to insert an appropriate acknowledgment in any subsequent printing.

Douglas Adams

Writer

Although Douglas Adams was actually born in Cambridge in 1952, he does not seem to have been able to recall his pre-Essex life. His parents split up in 1957, and his mother, Jan, a nurse, moved back in with her parents in Brentwood. His father, Christopher, a management consultant, remarried in 1960 and moved to Stondon Massey, just a few miles up the road. So from the age of five, Douglas and his younger sister Sue did a lot of to- and fro-ing from one parent to the other.

The two Essex families, and their lifestyles, were quite different. His Brentwood grandparents were an interesting pair: Grandpa Donovan was voluntarily bed-ridden, and Grandma Donovan took a whole host of unwell or injured animals into the house, playing havoc with Douglas's asthma. The house they lived in was small and – thanks in some part to his Grandma – crowded!

Douglas and Sue inherited two stepsisters and one half-sister from their father's new marriage, and Christopher and his growing family lived in a mock-Tudor pile with tennis courts, huge gardens, servants, and an Aston Martin in the garage. The new Mrs Adams was wealthy enough to be able to pay the fees for Douglas to attend the renowned Brentwood Preparatory School.

His exceptional height made Douglas stand out from the crowd, but, rather than the obvious choice of sporting pursuits, he was drawn to reading and creating stories. While at the prep school, he had an English class, taught by Frank Halford, where he was awarded the only ten out of ten of Halford's entire teaching career for a creative writing exercise. Douglas remembered this for the rest of his life.

Jan Adams re-married in 1964, providing two more half-siblings for the extended family. She moved to Dorset with her husband, a vet, meaning that Douglas switched from day boy to boarder after passing his eleven-plus with flying colours.

Although, in theory, his main aim in moving on to Cambridge University was to study English Literature, what he really wanted was to participate in the renowned Cambridge Footlights. He began writing revue material, and after five years was offered the chance to write some sketches for *Monty Python*.

After university, odd jobs – e.g. as a chicken-shed cleaner – kept him going while he wrote a series of scripts, some of which became the catalyst for his success. However, even when the radio series of *The Hitchhiker's Guide to the Galaxy* (based on his experiences hitch-hiking through Europe) was aired in 1978 after nine months' work, there was little indication that it would prove a life-changing event – he had been paid just £1,000. As a result, Douglas

Douglas Adams (left) with Terry Jones. (Courtesy of Pan Macmillan)

took a job as a BBC producer to ensure he had a wage. Six months later, he resigned to write the second radio series, the novel, the television series – and some episodes of *Doctor Who*. It was a workload all the more remarkable for someone with a legendary reputation for procrastination.

Regardless of his inability to meet deadlines, the *Hitchhiker's* series has sold over fifteen million copies. Any publisher would forgive a late manuscript for such a result ... Other novels, scripts, even a computer game, also did well.

On the personal front, Douglas married Jane Belson in 1991, a barrister with whom he had been involved on and off for nearly ten years. Their daughter Polly was born in 1994, and the family moved to Santa Barbara, California, in 1999. Following Douglas's untimely death at the age of forty-nine – a sudden, unexpected heart attack while at the gym – Jane and Polly returned to London.

Margery Allingham

Writer

Margery was actually born in West London in 1904, the eldest of three children. However, when she was only a few months old the family moved to the Old Rectory in Layer Breton, a remote village south west of Colchester on the edge of the Essex marshes.

Both her parents were prolific fiction writers, and she was encouraged to write by her father, who also supervised her education when illness kept her from attending school regularly. By the age of seven she could boast her own 'office' in the family home. Her first fee was for a story she wrote at the age of eight, which was published in one of the film journals that her Aunt Maud edited. From the age of eleven she was able to attend Endsleigh House School in Colchester for three years, moving on to a boarding school in Cambridge, and then to Regent Street Polytechnic (London) to study speech and drama – an effective way of dealing with a childhood stammer.

During that time several of Margery's stories had been published and her first novel, *Blackkerchief Dick*, appeared the year she left Regent Street Polytechnic (1923). Regent Street Polytechnic was also the place where she met the art student Philip (Pip) Youngman Carter. She had written a verse play, *Dido and Aeneas*, in which she played the leading role, and Pip designed the scenery. They married in 1927. It was Margery who was the prime bread-winner; Pip found it difficult to sell his art, but he helped Margery by producing covers and illustrations for her works, and after the Second World War he got a job writing for the *Tatler*.

In 1935 they settled at D'Arcy House at Tolleshunt D'Arcy, a few miles from Margery's childhood home. From here, she produced twenty-five novels, four novellas, sixty-four stories, numerous articles, and a wartime book about England (and especially Tolleshunt D'Arcy).

Albert Campion, her famous detective, made his first appearance in 1929 in *The Crime at Black Dudley*. Margery was at the forefront of the golden age of mystery writing, being a contemporary of Agatha Christie, Dorothy L. Sayers (who also lived in Essex as an adult) and Ngaio Marsh. Some of her dialogue shares its roots with another contemporary, P.G. Wodehouse, matching his eccentricity and wit. She introduces a comic manservant for Campion in *Mystery Mile* (1930) but Campion himself is an enigmatic figure, hinting at an aristocratic background. He proved her most successful creation, a creation which she developed in a series of novels, interrupted only by the war which saw her involved in first aid and air-raid work.

Margery's work was the forerunner of the kind of psychological interest which led to the novels of such writers as Ruth Rendell, P.D. James and Minette Walters. It was Margery who invented the urban serial-killer novel in *The Tiger in the Smoke* (1952), and this book attracted the most critical acclaim.

Margery Allingham. (Courtesy of the Margery Allingham Society)

In her work, there are examples of such universal problems as worship of money and masculinity in crisis – which could have been inspired by domestic problems with Pip's infidelities, the Inland Revenue pressing, and even perhaps their lack of children.

Not long after publishing *The Beckoning Lady*, with its autobiographical elements (1955) illness got the better of her. Finally, she succumbed to breast cancer, and died in Severalls Hospital in Colchester in 1966. Her grave is at St Nicholas' Church in Tolleshunt D'Arcy.

Posthumously, another novel was published (finished by Pip) in 1968 – *Cargo of Eagles*. Other work was adapted for cassette and for radio and in 1989/1990 a successful television series based on her novels attracted new readers. Peter Davison starred as Campion, with Brian Glover as his manservant.

Simon Amstell

Comedian and Television Presenter

Well known as a presenter on *Never Mind the Buzzcocks*, Simon Amstell is one of those individuals who has always known what he wanted to do, and has done it without wasting too much time. He was born in 1979 into a Jewish family in Gants Hill, Ilford, and went to Beal High School in Woodford Bridge Road.

His parents divorced in 1992, and (coincidentally?) Simon started doing stand-up a year later. He had already been attending drama classes on Saturday mornings, and acquired an early taste for applause in school shows. By the age of sixteen, Simon, who stayed with his mother at the Ilford family home, was writing short comic plays and skits.

Professionally, his first television appearance was in 1998 as a presenter on the children's channel Nickelodeon. He then presented *Popworld* on Channel 4 for six years, giving him time to develop his individual, ironic style, and giving the show a cult status. It seems he also realised during this period that he could develop an un-cool persona and still be funny, an approach which seems to have worked for him. Other presenting roles have been covering the Wireless Festival (Channel 4), the V Festival, and he has won Best Comedy Entertainment Personality at the British Comedy Awards and has been the youngest finalist of the BBC New Comedy Awards.

Simon also performs regularly on the stand-up circuit, selling out shows at the Edinburgh Fringe and turning up in places like the Palace Theatre, Westcliff-on-Sea and the Theatre Royal in London's Haymarket. With a regular BBC Radio 2 slot, you could say that this brands him as an establishment figure … but does an establishment figure tell jokes about being gay, about being a geek, about being from Essex, and about not being cool? Hardly.

Simon Amstell (centre), with Phill Jupitus (left) and Bill Bailey (right). (Author's Collection)

Trevor Bailey

Cricketer

Born in 1923, Leigh-on-Sea and its environs were, and are, home to Trevor Bailey. His father commuted from Fillebrook Avenue to the Admiralty, and Trevor and his older brother were able to amuse themselves – separately, in view of their eleven year age gap. For Trevor, such amusement was always sport, and especially cricket.

He went to local preparatory school, Alleyn Court, from the age of seven. His headmaster, Denys Wilcox, spotted his talent and Trevor earned his first XI colours aged nine in competition with thirteen-year-olds. His education continued at Dulwich College (South London) as a boarder, and he persuaded his family to move to the area, a move which coincided with the first blitz on the capital. Nevertheless, Trevor preferred life as a day-boy. By his second season at Dulwich, he was top of the batting and bowling averages.

In 1942, he was drafted into the Royal Marines, and commissioned. By the age of twenty-three, he was back at Alleyn Court as an assistant master, waiting to go to Cambridge University – and he had met his future wife, Greta. Before taking up his place at Cambridge, he had already played for Essex, but was seriously considering teaching, rather than pursuing cricket as a career. In 1948, he was offered the best of both worlds: a three year post as assistant secretary with Essex, which allowed him to play first-class cricket all summer, and increased his chances of an overseas tour with the MCC – plus he could go on teaching at Alleyn Court for two winters.

After making his mark with the Essex team as an all-rounder (including the rare feat of taking all ten wickets in an innings against Lancashire at Clacton), Trevor became a valuable member of England's squad from 1949. He was also playing football for amateur clubs Leytonstone and Walthamstow at this time. Perhaps his finest hour – or rather four hours – was that innings of 71 at Lord's against Australia in 1953 which (in partnership with Willie Watson) resulted in England going on to win the Ashes.

Trevor Bailey played in sixty-one Tests for England between 1949 and 1959, his bowling average was 29, his batting average was 30, and he took 32 catches. He captained Essex from 1961 to 1966, and in his twenty-one years for Essex he played 682 matches. Where records are concerned, he is the only player since the Second World War to score more than 2,000 runs in a season and take 100 wickets (1959). His wife, incidentally, was one of the first to accompany her husband on tour (in the 1950s), setting a precedent.

After his retirement in 1967, Trevor continued to play for Westcliff-on-Sea Cricket Club for many years, and became a cricket journalist and broadcaster. He was a regular on the BBC's *Test Match Special* for many years. From 1955, he was associated with the Ilford indoor cricket school, and much later with the Wrigley Soft Ball Cricket tournament for the very young, plus he has tried

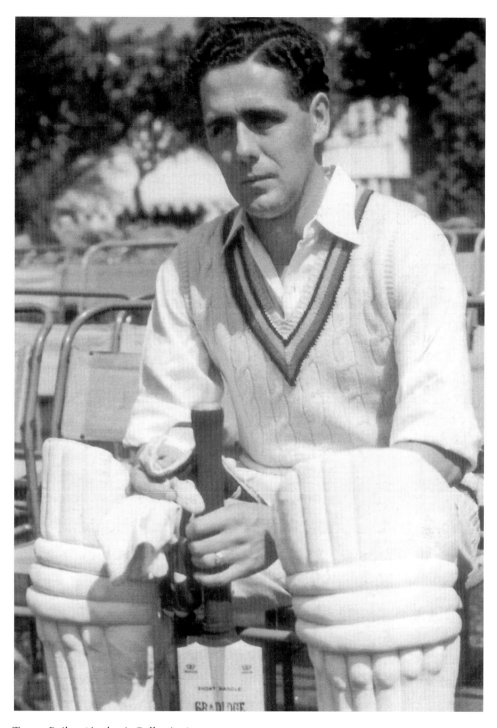

Trevor Bailey. (Author's Collection)

his hand at running sport shops in Essex. Sport, cricket, Essex and Trevor Bailey – the words are interchangeable. Now a grandfather (children Kim, Justin and Sharon were born in the 1950s), he remains a local legend.

Kenny Ball

Jazz Musician

One of nine children – although that included two adopted cousins – Kenny was born in Maysbrook Road, Dagenham, the youngest by ten years. He started school a little later than planned following a 10ft fall onto the sands at Southend-on-Sea when he was four (in 1934), which resulted in cerebrospinal fever.

The extended family moved house a couple of times during Kenny's childhood as his dad, a bookbinder, gained promotion. From the age of six to nine he lived in Worcestershire, where he first became attracted to the trumpet which featured in the sea cadets' band, Kenny being their mascot.

Back in Kinfauns Road, Goodmayes, in time for the Blitz, their new family home was near the railway line, clearly visible from the air, so they had an uncomfortable time of it for the next few years. Life, however, progressed, and Kenny, a pupil first at Chadwell Heath infants school and then at Mayfield Elementary, Ilford, joined the local sea cadets. Here, he learned to play the bugle, and bought his first trumpet second-hand from an advertisement in *Melody Maker* at the age of thirteen: it cost £10.

In 1944, Kenny left school and started working as a messenger for J. Walter Thompson in Berkeley Square, London. Much of his spare time was spent at Perrymans Farm Youth Club in May Street, Ilford, and at Ilford Palais. Here he could listen to music from local groups and even such luminaries as Ted Heath and his Band at the Palais, but his own beginnings were at the local St Margaret's Hall in Barking, jamming with local jazz bands. It was here where he met his first wife, Betty, when he was just sixteen, though they didn't marry for six years.

National Service came first, during which he spent two enjoyable years as a trainee electrician, based in Kent, but with some travel to Germany. He married Betty in 1952 at St Andrew's Church, Goodmayes, with a jamming session afterwards at their reception in Oakwood Gardens, the Ball family home. After a honeymoon in Weston-super-Mare they lived in one room in his sister's house at Seven Kings. Eventually, they managed to secure a mortgage on a terraced house in Goodmayes.

By now, Kenny had joined the Sid Phillips Dixieland Band, who kept him busy until he formed his own band, Kenny Ball and his Jazzmen, in 1958. Lonnie Donegan was instrumental, literally, in getting the band work on television and even in securing a recording contract for them. After the initial success of 'Samantha', Kenny earned a gold disc for 'Midnight in Moscow' (1961). That was the year they became the first traditional jazz band to appear at the London Palladium. Ten years later, with continued success, he had the ultimate accolade: an appearance on *This is Your Life*.

Kenny split from his wife and three children in 1978, partly due to their constant separation while he was touring. He had already met his next wife

Kenny Ball. (Courtesy of Kenny Ball Press Images)

by then, Michelle, although Betty was also ready to walk straight into another relationship. The marital home in Hornchurch was sold, but, with divorce costs and the cost of buying his ex-wife out of her shares in his Essex property investments, Kenny walked away with little to show for those successful years. He re-married in December 1983 at Hornchurch Register Office, economising on the reception by having it in the garage of the house where they were living.

Kenny has had more top 30 hits in the USA than Louis Armstrong, and gained honorary citizenship to the city of New Orleans. He can still sell out a venue, and currently lives in Essex with his wife in a seventeenth-century farmhouse near Stansted.

Raymond Baxter, OBE

Television Presenter

Raymond Baxter, he of the unmistakable voice, was born in 1922 and grew up in Wellesley Road, Ilford. His father was a science teacher and Raymond was educated at Ilford County High School. As a boy he was enthusiastic about cars, aeroplanes and music. He learned the violin and sang as a boy soprano, but it was when he took his first flight at the tender age of fourteen (with a pleasure trip on Alan Cobham's flying circus at a cost of 10s 6d) that he really got the flying bug.

In 1940 he joined the RAF (after a brief spell with the Water Board) and trained as a fighter pilot in Canada, before joining a squadron in Scotland for active service. He returned to England in 1944 to be an instructor and then a flight commander. He recommenced active service in September 1944 and his actions earned him several mentions in dispatches.

From 1945 to 1949 Raymond worked in Forces Broadcasting, joining the BBC in 1950. His most memorable radio commentaries were those on the funerals of Sir Winston Churchill and King George VI, and he also reported at such events as the Coronation of Queen Elizabeth II in 1953. Outstanding reportage during the 1960s included the first Concorde flight, the first Telstar broadcast, and an interview with Christian Barnard after the first heart transplant. As the BBC's prime outside broadcaster, he also reported live from the first passenger hovercraft crossing of the Channel in 1966.

As an accomplished rally driver (he competed in the Monte Carlo Rally twelve times), he frequently commentated on motoring – as well as aviation – events. As the BBC's motoring correspondent, he was commentator on twenty Formula 1 races, and he set the standard. For a remarkable thirty-six years until 1986, Raymond presented the BBC's coverage of the Farnborough Air Shows, nearly matching this with thirty years as a commentator on the Royal British Legion's annual Festival of Remembrance. He was the first reporter to broadcast from an aeroplane, an ocean liner – and even underwater.

After presenting a science series for four years (1959-1963), Raymond was given the opportunity to be the first host of what became the long-running *Tomorrow's World*. He worked on the programme for twelve years from July 1965 until he 'fell out' with the show's new editor in 1977. This show, which peaked with ten million viewers, emphasised the schoolboyish enthusiasm he felt for up-to-the-minute gadgetry. Among many 'marvels' – a favourite Raymond Baxter word – inventions he introduced were the electron microscope (1965), the breathalyser (1967), the pocket calculator (1971), and the barcode reader.

By now, Raymond was living in a comfortable Queen Anne house with a 32-acre garden at Denham in Buckinghamshire. His departure from *Tomorrow's World* coincided with a tribunal about the sacking of his gardener for alleged incompetence. The gardener, required to leave a tied cottage, claimed unfair dismissal but lost his case. The court appearance left its mark. A year later Raymond sold up and moved to a more modest home in Henley with his family: American wife Sylvia, son and daughter.

Away from broadcasting, Raymond became vice president of the Royal National Lifeboat Institution in 1987, was a founder member of the Association of Dunkirk Little Ships (as an owner of one of the vessels) and eventually its honorary admiral, plus honorary chairman of the Royal Aeronautical Society from 1991. He was made an Honorary Freeman of the City of London in 1978, and awarded the OBE in 2003. Surviving his wife by ten years – they were married for fifty – Raymond Baxter died at the Royal Berkshire Hospital in Reading in 2006, but his ground-breaking work will ensure that he will live on in the archives of the BBC's history.

Raymond Baxter.
(Author's Collection)

Nigel Benn

Boxer

There are a number of boxers who have taken up residence in Essex in adulthood and become associated with the county, but Nigel Benn was brought up on the streets of Ilford. He went to school at Loxford.

It seems that Nigel, born in 1964, the sixth of seven sons, regarded big brother, Andy, as his role model. Andy, in and out of borstal, earned respect on the streets for the way he handled himself. But, when Nigel was eight, Andy fell through a conservatory roof and died from his injuries. Nigel, devastated, stepped into his shoes.

The Army instilled in him some sense of direction. He signed on at sixteen, joining the 1st Battalion of the Royal Regiment of Fusiliers where he honed his boxing skills. His temperament was hardened by two tours of Northern Ireland during the height of the troubles. In the Army, Nigel was unbeatable in the boxing ring, and he turned professional in 1987 after forty-one wins and one loss as an amateur.

His first match resulted in a second round knock-out, and was followed by twenty-one similar fights, over half of them finishing in the first round. During his first professional year he was awarded the Young Boxer of the Year title, and his powerful punch earned Nigel his nickname: The Dark Destroyer. From April to November 1990, he was WBO Middleweight Champion, and between 1992 and 1996 he was the WBC Super Middleweight Champion. In 1995, his most brutal match resulted in Gerald McLellan being permanently paralysed and blind.

Once he hit the big time, Nigel succumbed to every temptation available (especially to those in the public eye): drink, women, drugs and every cheap, and not so cheap, thrill. When he took an overdose of sleeping tablets in 1998, his wife Carolyne felt that only the church could change all this, and it seems she was right. His first wife, Sharron, had chosen a different solution: divorce.

Since leaving boxing, Nigel has made an equal impact in the world of the media, featuring in *I'm a Celebrity … Get Me Out of Here!* in which he raised funds for the NSPCC, and in Channel 5's *Gladiator*.

Away from a sometimes critical public gaze, Nigel is a devoted family man. His wife and his children, Dominic, Sade, Renee, Conor and India, are the main focus of his life. Nigel is now a born-again preacher, living since 2002 in a mansion on the Costa de la Calma in Majorca, with a Sunday congregation of three dozen. He cooks for local pensioners, and is interested in missionary work.

Nigel Benn. (Author's Collection)

Lord Sidney Bernstein

Television Baron

Alexander Bernstein, Sidney's father, had moved to Ilford from Sweden at the end of the nineteenth century; his shoemaking business had failed when his contract to supply boots to the Boers collapsed when the Boer War broke out. With family assistance, Alexander bought land first in Ilford and then in North London, and built the first of the Bernstein theatres, the Edmonton Empire, in 1908, which was run like a music hall. The official opening on Boxing Day was attended by the Bernstein children in their sailor suits, handing out sweets to local children as they filed in to see such delights as the troupe of elephants.

Sidney was born in 1899, the fourth of nine children, and remembers living at Cleodora House, Bathurst Road, Ilford, which had a garden that ran down to the River Roding with the green stretches of Ilford golf course beyond. As children multiplied and finances grew, the family moved into ever larger houses, always in Ilford. Their home was Orthodox Jewish, and a rabbi visited to teach the children Hebrew. There was no synagogue in the vicinity, and they had to walk several miles to one in Romford at the weekends. School was the Highlands School in Ilford and then a scholarship secured him a place at Cooper's Company School in Bow, East London.

It seems that Sidney was not averse to playing truant on occasion – the first film he escaped to see was the funeral of Edward VII, and he also absented himself occasionally to visit the Ilford Hippodrome. By the time Sidney left school, at fifteen, the family had moved again – to Cricklewood in North London.

In 1915, Sidney's elder brother, Selim, was killed at Gallipoli, after having joined up despite the anti-Semitic mood then prevalent. Sidney tried hard to join up, but was prevented from doing so by surgery he had had on his nose to improve his breathing after a football injury, which rendered him 'permanently and totally disabled for service'.

When his father died in 1922, Sidney took over the family business. He concentrated on the film theatre business, but also loved live theatre and tried several ventures at the Court Theatre and Phoenix Theatres in London. Film seemed to him more profitable and he was a founder member of the British Film Society in 1924; he introduced Saturday morning matinées for children in 1927; he acquired control of some thirty cinemas by the late 1930s; and he became chairman of the Granada Group in 1934. By the end of the '30s, Sidney Bernstein was a powerful force in the film and television industry, with burgeoning publishing involvement. In 1956 Sidney, along with his brother Cecil, founded Granada Television. Granada's biggest single success is of course *Coronation Street*, which has been on air since 1960.

Cinema continued to play a part in Sidney Bernstein's career. He was chief of the film section in the Allied Forces in the Second World War against the advice of MI5 who regarded him – with his communist friends – as a security risk. In 1948, he and Alfred Hitchcock formed Transatlantic Pictures (Sidney produced some of Hitchcock's films).

Marriage to Zoe in 1936 ended in divorce in the early '50s. He married Sandra in 1954 at the Dorchester Hotel – she was twenty-four years his junior. Both weddings had been low profile events. Marriage to Sandra gave him a step-daughter, Charlotte, followed by son (David) and daughter (Jane) for the family-loving Sidney.

His biggest honour came in 1969 when he was created Baron Bernstein of Leigh. Other honours included Fellowship of the British Film Institute and an International Emmy Directorate Award in 1984. Lord Sidney Bernstein died at his London home in 1993 (of cerebral arteriosclerosis), two years after the unexpected death of Sandra. He was a spectacularly successful Essex entrepreneur.

Sidney Bernstein. (Courtesy of Caroline Moorehead)

Ursula Bloom

Writer

Ursula fills the Essex criteria because although she left the county at an early age, she returned to spend many later years in the county. She was born in 1892 in Springfield, Chelmsford where her father was the curate of Springfield.

The family started moving around when Ursula was just two, so that she spent her youth in various rectories, notably one at Whitchurch, near Stratford-upon-Avon. Ursula was home educated, and published her first book, *Tiger*, at the age of seven. She was also taught the piano and the violin.

It does seem that, in spite of his status, her father was a serial womaniser, and this may well have been behind some of their moves. Before the First World War her mother left him, and moved with Ursula and younger brother Joscelyn to St Albans, where they were less financially stable. Young Ursula brought in some money by playing the piano at the local cinema. By 1914, they had found a rented house in what they regarded as a healthier climate: Saville Street in Walton (or Walton-on-the-Naze).

Ursula married Captain Arthur Brownlow Denham-Cookes in 1916, a man who could offer her a more comfortable lifestyle. They took a furnished house – called 'Poona' – on the seafront at Frinton-on-Sea with ten bedrooms and servants, and her mother moved to rooms nearby. Sadly, Arthur died in 1918 – of influenza – shortly after she had given birth to their son, Pip.

Newly single and still in her twenties, Ursula enjoyed dancing the night away with a gang of post-war young things, but she also found time to produce her first novel, *The Great Beginning* (published in 1924). She was also a fan of cycling – and naturism! Her second husband was Commander Charles Gower Robinson, RN, and they married in 1925 with a wedding reception at the Beach House Hotel in Frinton.

Frinton before the Second World War was a place growing in popularity with Londoners. Temporary residents included Gladys Cooper and Douglas Fairbanks, and visitors included Winston Churchill, Noel Coward and Ivor Novello. However, naval families had to get used to moving around. The family seem to have spent time in Epping and then settled in Harlow in 'the coldest house in England,' where Pip went to Harlow College. After the Second World War, the family invested in a bungalow built on two plots of land near to Frinton station.

By the 1930s Ursula was also writing features for nationals such as the *Sunday Pictorial* and *Woman's Own*, and she was variously a crime reporter and an agony aunt. In spite of this, her output as a novelist was prolific and she was in the *Guinness Book of Records* for a while as the most prolific female writer. She wrote readable romances, historical novels, hospital novels, biographies and non-fiction, the latter incorporating such subjects as needlework, religion, cookery, beauty and careers, as well as her own family history. One relevant title in 1970 was *Rosemary for Frinton*.

Ursula Bloom. (Author's Collection)

Apparently one of her journalistic coups – in the 1950s – was to discover the whereabouts of Ethel Le Neve (Dr Crippen's mistress) who was living as a housewife in Croydon. Ursula even found time to produce radio and stage plays.

In her lifetime, she produced over 560 books, using a variety of pseudonyms including Lozania Prole, Mary Essex, Rachel Harvey, Deborah Mann, Sheila Burns and Sara Sloane. This meant she was writing around ten books a year, her last being *Sweet Spring of April* which was published in 1979, the year her husband died.

By 1983, she was one of the few authors earning the maximum possible under the Public Lending Right scheme based on borrowings from public libraries. A year later, Ursula Bloom died (in Hampshire, although she had also lived in Sussex), a literary record breaker that Essex can justifiably claim as its own.

Tim Bowler

Writer

Tim Bowler. (Courtesy of Oxford University Press)

Born in 1953 and brought up in Leigh-on-Sea, Tim went to Westcliff High School for Boys. The house he grew up in overlooked the Thames Estuary, which became the background for his first novel, *Midget*. His parents had a boat which they sailed regularly, developing his interest in sailing and the sea.

At home, the influences were more musical than literary, so he discovered William Blake on his own; his taste even then was for the mystical. His interest at school was in languages rather than literature, and he read Swedish and Scandinavian Studies at the University of East Anglia, living for a while in Sweden. After working in a variety of jobs, including the timber and forestry trades, he returned to Britain to teach. Writing, however, was always hovering on the brink of his ambitions, having written his first story at the age of five.

Midget was written over a ten-year period, mostly in the early mornings before going out to work. A move to Newton Abbot in Devon was the result of being offered a job as Head of Modern Languages, but in 1990 he left teaching to become a full-time writer and translator.

Tim won the 1998 Carnegie Medal with his third novel, *River Boy*, a prestigious award which changed his life in many ways. He has gone on to win the Angus Book Award and the Lancashire Libraries Children's Book Award for *Shadows*, his fourth novel, with his fifth (*Storm Catchers*) winning the South Lanarkshire Book Award and the Stockton Libraries Award. *Shadows*, incidentally, features fiercely competitive squash matches, reflecting Tim's own experience of league squash for Totnes over twenty years.

Apart from twelve books, often regarded as crossover novels because of their all-age appeal, but generally pigeonholed as 'children's' books, he has more recently been working on a series of thrillers entitled *Blade*, which he describes as an urban journey to redemption. The third and fourth in the series will be released in 2009.

He lives in Devon with his wife, Rachel, a teacher he met when they were both studying at UEA. However, he still retains a fondness for Leigh-on-Sea, and would dearly love to see a film crew in the area, shooting *Midget*, a psychic and psychological thriller.

His website, it has to be said, makes his writing life look pretty much idyllic with pictures of the stone outhouse where he works and his descriptions of the surrounding countryside. But Tim returns to Essex frequently not only to visit family but to look in on schools in the area, and talk about his books and his chosen profession, inspiring students with his enthusiasm. Tim Bowler is a story teller first, a crusader second, and succeeds with both.

Billy Bragg

Musician

The Bard of Barking first made his presence felt, as Stephen William Bragg, a few days before Christmas in Upney Hospital in 1957. His father was from Essex stock; his mother the grand-daughter of an Italian immigrant who had settled in the East End.

Billy recalls boyhood holidays at Shoeburyness, where he was a fan of the beaches, and where his dad allowed him to drive their green Morris Oxford around the car park. A chalet at St Osyth, near Clacton, belonging to a family friend, also figures in his childhood memories.

He lived with his brother and parents in a house called 'Stanley' and next door, in 'Livingstone', lived the Wigg family. Philip Wigg (or Wiggy) and Billy went to Northbury junior school and then to Park Modern secondary school, as had their fathers before them. Billy and Wiggy and their guitars had the beginnings of a band.

For those locals who failed their eleven plus, the nearest equivalent of further education was at the nearby Ford production plant. Billy avoided the temptation, having had a taste of fame reading out an early poem on Radio Essex at the age of just thirteen. Instead, he bucked the system by securing an office job at Overseas Containers in Barking – but only for six months because he wanted to spend some time in France. Another job, in a London bank this time, paid for suits and records (The Small Faces were a favourite) as his interest in music developed.

The two teenagers were joined by other Essex lads, Robert (a punk trainee undertaker who became the drummer) and Ricey (Stephen Rice) on keyboards. A name, Riff Raff, emerged in 1977. Gigs were regular, but not that well paid, so the boys kept their day jobs. Songs at the time included such gems as 'Romford Girls'.

What Billy really wanted to do, as a confirmed Socialist, was to change the world. So he switched tactics for a while and joined the Army (1981) and followed his father's wartime footsteps by choosing the Royal Armoured Corps. After three months, he bought himself out, but the experience has stayed with him – all experiences were grist to his songwriter's mill. His songs represent a combination of folk, poetry and social comment.

Gradual popularity within a group and as a solo act led to his first recording contract in 1983. *Brewing up with Billy Bragg*, released in 1984, included the type of material with which he was to become associated – criticising Margaret Thatcher and the popular press, and paying tribute to Falklands heroes. He went on to produce a number of rallying cries for the Labour movement, but switched to more specific issues of social injustice as the years passed. There isn't enough space here to list all his songs, his albums, his journalistic credits and his soundtrack work, although there is room to mention his book: *The Progressive Patriot*.

Billy and his partner, Julie, had a son, Jack on the 27 December 1993, cementing their relationship. (Billy also has a stepson, Jamie). In 1999 there was a different kind of excitement – cutting the ribbon at the entrance to Bragg Close, Barking. Billy claims that his reaction to any rock ego is likely to be: 'You might be in the rock'n'roll hall of fame, mate, but I'm in the *A to Z!*' He must be equally proud to be currently singing with Ian McLagan (ex Small Faces, his early heroes) as part of his touring band, The Blokes.

The Braggs saw in the new millennium on the Dorset coast where they had invested in a picturesque property near the village of Burton Bradstock. Since then he has been as happy to do charity gigs in his adopted village to raise money for the local scout hut as he has been to tour Europe, Australia and America. But his Essex roots live on in such lyrics as: *If you ever go to Shoeburyness, Take the A-road, the OK-road, that's the best – go motoring on the A13* (from *A13, Trunk Road to the Sea*).

Billy Bragg. (Photograph by Wiggy)

Russell Brand

Actor and Comedian

In 1975, after just six months in the world, Russell became the product of a one-parent family, when his father Ronald, a photographer, promptly left. He was an only child, and he lived with his mother, Barbara, in Grays, Essex. His dad was very much a weekend father, with Russell spending time at his dad's bachelor pad in Brentwood, watching comedy videos. They also managed a few annual father-and-son trips to West Ham.

To offset the lack of maintenance forthcoming from her ex, his mother had a number of jobs, selling dishwashers, or waitressing. As a youngster, Russell's favourite haunt was the local abandoned barracks, handy for collecting newts, and his holiday destination was usually Pontin's.

Orsett Hospital, where he was born, was also the place where his mother started receiving cancer treatment in 1982. At the time, Russell was at Little Thurrock Primary, but not long afterwards, his father – temporarily flush with money – funded Russell's education at Gidea Park College, where he needed some private tuition to help him keep up with the other pupils. When his mum was in remission, Russell was offered a scholarship at Hockeril, a state run boarding school in Hertfordshire, and she encouraged him in his independence.

Against his better judgment, they did manage to instil a decent education into him, until he was expelled (after a girl was found under his bed) and he returned to Grays Comprehensive.

This was a luckier break than it seemed, because now he found he was actually enjoying school – or at least the drama lessons; and he made his debut on stage as Fat Sam in the school's version of *Bugsy Malone*. He was actually overweight at the time, which may have helped with the casting. Russell also managed to get some work as an extra through the advertisements that appeared in the back pages of *The Stage*. He then auditioned for the Italia Conti stage school, joining them at sixteen, before studying for three years at the Drama Centre in Chalk Farm from where he was expelled after a few drug-related run-ins with the law.

Comedy now beckoned. He lived in his grandmother's house in Dagenham for a while, and then in North London, while his career – and his drug-taking – blossomed. Starting with pubs and clubs on the outer London fringes, the Hackney Empire, and the Edinburgh Festival, his success led to his being offered a regular presenting spot on MTV which financed his heroin addiction. He was sacked after going to work dressed as Osama Bin Laden the day after 9/11.

Russell's radio work has included XFM, BBC6 Music and a late-night slot on Radio 2. Since MTV he has hosted *Big Brother's Big Mouth*, presented *Kings of Comedy* (E4) and had his own chat show on Channel 4. He has also appeared in ITV's *The Abbey* as a recovering crack addict; he has been clean since 2003 thanks to pressure from his manager.

His stand-up won him Best Newcomer at the 2006 British Comedy Awards and 2007 saw him hosting the Brit Awards. More ambitiously (and more recently), Russell made a successful comedy film debut in *St Trinian's* as Flash Harry, moving on to a Hollywood role as a rock star in *Forgetting Sarah Marshall*, where some critics felt he stole the show.

He has other claims to fame – he was voted 'sexiest vegetarian' in PETA Europe's 2007 poll and the worst dressed *and* the most stylish man (*GQ Magazine* 2008) and he is patron of the drug addiction charity Focus 12.

Whatever Russell does, he seems to end up in a confrontational situation, as in the highly publicised telephone call to Andrew Sachs. Russell's subsequent resignation from the BBC should do his career no harm.

Russell Brand. (Photograph by Sandra Phillips. http://fun-autographs.tripod.com)

Martina Cole

Writer

Martina was born into a large Irish Catholic family in Aveley, South Essex, in 1959, and went to a convent school. However, she was expelled for smoking, allegedly dated a bank robber at fourteen, and she was married at sixteen. At the other end of the spectrum, she was an avid reader while at school.

Her first pay-packet, at sixteen, was £11 for a week's work as a typist in the West End of London. By the age of nineteen, she was divorced, a punk with pink hair and a baby son, living in an unfurnished flat on a council estate in Tilbury. To support them, she had tried waitressing, supermarket work and agency nursing locally to save the fares. Martina also tells a story of dressing son Christopher as a punk and taking him to the Tower of London so that Japanese tourists would take pictures of them – for a £10 fee ...

To entertain herself in the absence of a television, she completed her first novel, *Dangerous Lady*, by the time she was twenty-one. It was written almost as a reaction against the sex-and-shopping books that were so popular at the time. Nearly a decade later, she realised that it was never going to get anywhere by being left in a drawer, and she spent the best part of a tax rebate on a £200 electric typewriter and reworked the whole story into a publishable form. The agent she sent it to, Darley Anderson, invited her for lunch and told her the book was going to auction. Martina, in her naivety, thought this was the normal way that books were published, and she was anticipating 'as much as £3,000'. Imagine her reaction when Darley Anderson telephoned to say he'd secured her a £150,000 advance! Even Anderson admitted that it was the biggest advance he had ever secured. *Dangerous Lady* went on to become a successful television drama.

Her successes since that first novel have been phenomenal, and the sales of her books show no signs of slowing down. She was the top-selling adult-fiction author in Britain in 2005 and 2006, she has won the Crime Thriller of the Year award (2006), she is published in twenty-eight languages, and her back-catalogue alone sells 10,000 books a week in the UK. Hardback sales for a new novel by Martina Cole can easily reach 400,000. In 2006, she secured an unprecedented seven-figure advance for a four book deal with Headline, her publishers. 2008 saw the publication of her fourteenth novel, *Faces*.

As a writer, she is highly acclaimed for her gutsy, compelling and hard-hitting story-lines and style. The focus on criminal activity and harsh lives is what her readers obviously love, although her books are ultimately redemptive. She is a hit in British prisons, and her books are stolen more than any others from Essex and East London bookshops. Contrarily, she also has fans in the police force.

The first property Martina bought was in the early 1980s – a cottage in West Thurrock which cost £17,000. Nowadays, she is worth in excess of £20 million. She has her own television production company and has actually moved away from her roots to Kent. Now divorced from her second husband, Martina lives with her daughter Freddie, the 1996 fruit of this marriage. She is happier with a housekeeper than a husband, because men eventually 'get on her nerves.'

Her lifestyle allows her to indulge her love of expensive handbags and luggage, but it hasn't all been roses. Martina had a cancerous tumour on her leg when she was pregnant the second time, and she has had to live with painful rheumatoid arthritis. In spite of her move away from Essex, she keeps in touch with her roots – it's what she's all about. She has even been seen signing books at Romford Market.

Martina Cole.
(Photograph by Sandra Phillips. http://fun-autographs.tripod.com)

Bernard Cornwell, OBE

Writer

The London-born author of the *Sharpe* novels was given up for adoption in 1944 at the age of two weeks. His single mother gave birth in a Hackney institution, and his father, William Oughtred, a Canadian airman, did not stick around.

The Wiggins family from Thundersley took him in and changed his name from Bernard Cornwell (his mother's surname) to Wiggins. They adopted five children in all, and the family were brought up to believe that if they kept themselves separate from a sinful world, they might attain salvation. This was the concept of the sect to which his new parents belonged: the Leigh-on-Sea branch of the Peculiar People. The Peculiars were fundamentalists who disapproved of alcohol, cigarettes, make-up, television, cinema, gambling, dancing, conventional medicine, and toys such as guns. Could this explain Bernard's early interest in CS Forester's *Hornblower* novels, and his fascination for military adventure?

Interestingly, he was sent to Monkton Combe School in Bath, a Christian boarding school, rather than being educated locally. It seems that Marjorie Wiggins loved babies, but was not quite so keen on children. Worse, Joseph Wiggins was rather too fond of wielding a bamboo garden stake on the bare flesh of his adopted family if they transgressed. As an adult, Bernard is not in touch with his remaining adopted 'siblings' and, after Joseph died, he changed his name back to Cornwell.

Wanting to escape such strictures, and having failed his eyesight test for the Army, he opted to study theology at London University. However, he ended up joining the BBC's *Nationwide* team, working his way up the ladder to become head of current affairs at BBC Northern Ireland. Judy, his future American wife, was then working at Thames TV in Belfast, where they met. She was unable to stay in the UK for family reasons but they married in 1980, aiming to live and work in the USA. Unfortunately (or perhaps not …) Bernard was unable to get a Green Card, so he decided to write – and Richard Sharpe, soldier from a fictional South Essex regiment, was born. Bernard admits that even he, since the advent of Sean Bean in the title role, thinks that Sean epitomises Richard Sharpe.

Bernard Cornwell is now an American citizen, but still visits these shores to promote new books. When appearing at such events as the annual Essex Book Festival, he has admitted to fond memories of sailing on the River Crouch and the Blackwater. Nowadays, however, he divides his time between homes in Cape Cod and South Carolina. He is also the owner of two boats, including a 24ft Cornish crabber, the *Royalist,* on which he spends at least two months of the year.

Apart from *Sharpe*, other successes have included the Arthurian *Warlord Chronicles*, the *Starbuck Chronicles* about the American Civil War, and the

Saxon Stories about King Arthur. Altogether, his tally is approaching fifty novels, with the added bonus of their popularity on screen. Bernard's work has sold five million copies in nine languages, and he is arguably the most popular writer of historical fiction in the UK.

In 2006, he received the accolade of OBE for services to 'literature and television production'. It is interesting to speculate whether the OBE, Sharpe, or even Bernard Cornwell, the writer, would ever have happened without that Essex beginning.

Bernard Cornwell. (Courtesy Bernard Cornwell)

Alan Davies

Actor and comedian

Stand-up comedian, actor, raconteur, with success on stage, radio and television, Alan Davies (born in 1966) has pursued his ambition from his school days, and has proved what talent and determination can do.

Alan Davies. (Courtesy MF Management)

He is the product of a mainly one parent family, his mother Shirley having died from leukaemia when he was just six. He and his older brother and younger sister were brought up by their father. Alan did him proud at school, achieving eight GCE O-levels at Bancroft's School in Woodford Green, and four further O-levels plus two A-levels (Media and Theatre Studies) at Loughton College of Further Education. He went on to study drama and theatre at Kent University. This is where he seems to have become involved in the CND.

To pursue his comedy ambitions, he moved to Stoke Newington for a while, with his first gig there at the Black Cat. It seems that he was funded in his career path by the government's Enterprise Allowance Scheme – very enterprising. In 1991, he won the *Time Out* Award for Best Comic and his career began to take off. He became a regular on the alternative circuit, appearing alongside such peers as Eddie Izzard and David Baddiel.

In 1994, he was nominated for the Perrier Award at the Edinburgh Fringe and a year later, another nomination was for best stand up in the British Comedy Awards.

Turning up at a BBC party in his (now) famous duffle coat when being considered for *Jonathan Creek* apparently secured him the part, and from 1997 the series was a ratings success, and is still being shown on satellite channels. While *Jonathan Creek* won a BAFTA for best drama, Alan had his own radio show in 1998, having already made an appearance on *Have I Got News For You*. He presented a documentary series on stand-up comedians in 2000 and had a cameo role in *Dog Eat Dog* – a British film released in 2001. Since then he has starred in *Bob and Rose* and *The Brief* for ITV.

More recently, Alan's face is familiar as a panellist on the BBC's *QI* show. However, his most lucrative contract was probably for the Abbey National advertisements, which earned him well over £1 million.

After a stormy couple of on-and-off years with Julia Sawalha, Alan married literary agent Kate Maskell in 2007 and the couple live in Highbury, North London, in an up-market town house. He likes the area because it is within walking distance of the Arsenal ground and there are over eighty restaurants between his home and the Angel – although not all would appeal to someone of his vegetarian persuasion.

Robert Daws

Actor

Born in 1959, the first five years of Robert's life were spent in and out of Rochford Hospital on the Southend-on-Sea borders. He was born with two club feet, resulting in numerous operations. As a child, he lived with his family (including three younger siblings) in a chalet in Leigh-on-Sea.

After completing his education at Belfairs High School in Leigh, Robert studied drama at the Royal Academy of Dramatic Art. He made his acting debut as the back end of a camel in *Aladdin* at the Palace Theatre in Westcliff-on-Sea, collecting £17.50 for his first week's wages. It seems he was so excited by the event that it took him a week to open the little brown envelope containing his pay.

Robert Daws. (Courtesy Celebrity Productions)

As his experience has grown, so has the amount of work he has been offered. Robert has worked pretty much non-stop since the mid-1980s. Early television work then included *Robin of Sherwood* and *Casualty*, with roles in *Jeeves and Wooster*, *Lovejoy*, *The House of Elliott*, *Roger Roger* and *Outside Edge* in the 1990s. The twenty-first century has seen him become a recognisable face and he has featured even more prominently in such series as *Heartbeat*, *Midsomer Murders*, and, especially, *The Royal*. His film credits include *Arthur's Dyke*.

Robert married Amanda Waring in 1993 and they had one son, Benjamin, who has appeared as 'a hippy child' in an episode of *The Royal*. They divorced in 2002 and Robert subsequently married Amy Robbins (Dr Weatherill in *The Royal*) who he met on set. They now have two daughters – Betsy and May. The couple have a base in London.

Apart from repertory theatre credits, Robert has been offered so much television work that he has had little time for stage work. Nevertheless, he did return for only the second time in eighteen years to play a leading role in a dramatic two-hander with *Monarch of the Glen*'s Dawn Steele in *A Blackbird with Bite*, a disturbing, hard-hitting play about obsessive love. Although he described it as 'a monster of a play to learn' it has had a successful tour from 2007 through to 2008. Behind the scenes, he was joint artistic director of Southern Lights at the New End Theatre, Hampstead for over two years.

Robert has been a regular broadcaster on BBC Radio Four, most recently as Inspector Trueman in three series of *Trueman and Riley*. He has also appeared in a one-man show, *Summoned by Betjeman*, a self-devised tribute to John Betjeman's writing. No longer just regarded as a 'comedy' actor, Robert is going from strength to strength.

Darren Day

Actor and Singer

Born and educated in Colchester, Darren Day (born Darren Graham in 1968) went to Sir Charles Lucas Art College. As a youngster, he excelled in music, drama, athletics and snooker – in fact he became a semi-professional snooker player on leaving school. Some of his family still live in the Colchester area, and Darren also spent part of his formative years in Billericay.

As an all-round entertainer, including a talent for impressions, he toured the club circuit in the '80s, and even did a stint as a Butlin's redcoat, but got his first big break in 1993 when he took over from Philip Schofield in *Joseph and the Amazing Technicolor Dreamcoat*. Since then he has hosted television shows such as *You Bet*, released a solo album, and has appeared in pantomime as well as a variety of other musicals, e.g. *Summer Holiday*, *Grease*, *The Rocky Horror Show*, *Hello Dolly*, *Carousel*, and *Copacabana*. Reality show viewers will have spotted him in *I'm a Celebrity … Get me Out of Here!*, and *Celebrity Scissorhands*.

Lovers of gossip will also know his name just as well from his well-documented colourful love life. He could probably enter the *Guinness Book of Records* for the record number of 'engagements' he has had, and his relationship with Suzanne Shaw (winner of 2008's *Celebrity Dancing on Ice*) resulted in the birth of their son Corey in 2004. Darren finally succumbed to marriage in 2007, when his wedding to actress Stephanie Dooley took place in Comlongon Castle in Dumfries. They had met when on stage in *Cinderella* together the previous year. Committed at last, Darren dressed for this very special day in a kilt as a tribute to his late, Glaswegian, father. Stephanie's eight-year-old son and the couple's baby daughter (Madison Angel) were at the ceremony, where white doves were released in a very romantic setting.

Following some straight dramatic roles – on stage in *Alfie* and in television's *The Bill* and *Doctors* for example – Darren, it seems, has ambitions to do more serious work. It appears that he wants to escape the sort of unsavoury attention that his 'love-rat' reputation earned him, not to mention the stories about his drinking and his expensive cocaine addiction which led to his 2006 bankruptcy.

Darren has settled in Barnsley, Yorkshire, with his new family, not far from his new in-laws. Hopefully, these new responsibilities will help him to achieve his worthy aims, a long way – in every way – from his council estate beginning.

Darren Day. (Author's Collection)

Basil Dearden

Film Director

Basil Dearden, from *Film Dope* magazine April 1976. (Author's Collection)

A successful film director, Basil Dear was born in 1911 in Woodfield Road, Southend, one of six children. His father was an electrical engineer who died at sea during the First World War. As a result, his widowed mother, Dorothy, had a difficult task bringing up such a large family in the days before benefit systems were in place.

He left school early to bring in some money for the family, working in a London insurance company. However, three of his siblings became involved in the theatre, and he too became interested, starting with walk on amateur parts, and then joining the Grand Theatre, Fulham (London) as an assistant stage manager.

At the age of twenty-one, Basil became production manager for impresario Basil Dean and changed his name to Dearden to avoid confusion. Dean became head of Ealing Studios and Basil (Dearden) turned his hand to writing, producing, and, ultimately, directing. By 1938, he was working with Ealing's top comedy stars, such as George Formby and Will Hays.

His first work as sole director was *The Bells Go Down* (1943) celebrating the heroes of the Auxiliary Fire Service during the Blitz. *The Blue Lamp*, one of his most famous films which introduced *Dixon of Dock Green*, was made towards the end of the Ealing period, in 1950. Together with Michael Relph, the duo created a partnership which lasted nearly thirty years, and opened up new social commentary themes not tackled before in British films, such as homosexuality. They worked on comedies, dramas and murder mysteries.

Melissa Stribling, an actress who had appeared in four of his films, became Basil's wife in the 1940s, and they had two sons, James (1949) and Torquil (1959). Melissa seems to have specialised in horror films and comedies, James grew up to follow in his father's footsteps as writer-director and Torquil moved into editing.

As for Basil himself, by the 1960s, he was working on controversial films such as *Victim* (1961) and large-scale action films, the most famous being *Khartoum* in 1966. His last film was *The Man Who Haunted Himself* (1970) with Roger Moore.

Just one year later, Basil was in a road accident while driving back from Pinewood to his Belgravia home, and was declared dead at Hillingdon Hospital. Melissa survived him for a number of years. (Her last film was *Paris by Night* released in 1988, while James's most famous piece of work is probably *Fatal Attraction* in 1987 which gave him an Oscar nomination for his screenplay.)

(George) Warwick Deeping

Writer

Not as well known in the twenty-first century as in the twentieth, Warwick Deeping was the author of over sixty best-selling novels, several collections of short stories and several plays. He was born in 1877 in Prospect House, Southend-on-Sea, opposite the Royal Hotel at the top of Pier Hill. The house later became the Royal Oyster Saloon, then a fishing tackle store, but has now been replaced with The Royals Shopping Complex. Later he lived literally yards away at No. 19 Royal Terrace where he had a view of the (then) wooden pier.

His writing reveals happy memories of his childhood which he describes as being 'nearer to nature than many modern children ... gorged on municipal pleasures'. A pre-breakfast swim was part of his routine, and he recalls when The Shrubbery between Royal Terrace and the seafront had green-coated guardians. He also remembers skating on the pond at Porter's (now the mayor's house).

George's father, uncle and grandfather were well known in the town. They were all doctors, his father having played a prominent part in establishing the old Victoria Hospital which was in Warrior Square. Following in the family footsteps Warwick also trained as a doctor at the Middlesex Hospital in London after completing his education at Trinity College where he gained his MA. However, his interest in literature soon took over from medicine; this probably did not go down too well at home. He published his first novel, *Uther and Igraine*, in 1903, which achieved modest success, and continued writing full time until joining the Army Medical Corps in 1915, seeing active service at Gallipoli as captain.

Having married Phyllis Merril, a captain's daughter, in 1904, he moved to Weybridge in Surrey after the war and his military experiences turned his literary attentions to more contemporary themes. His most popular book, *Sorrell and Son* (later televised), was said to be based on Southend and his experiences in the war. This was his thirty-third novel, and his publishers, Cassell, prided themselves on producing an annual spring or autumn 'Deeping' for all his fans. Four other novels (*Caroline Terrace, The Dark House, Slade* and *Mr Gurney and Mr Slade*) deal with the locality of Southfleet, a probable disguise for Southend. Many of his books were published in America and Australia, and a number were translated into several languages. His range covered subjects as diverse as Roman Britain and the Middle Ages, and five novels were adapted for the big screen.

He died in 1950 and six books were published posthumously between 1952 and 1957, indicating his prolific ability. He is buried in St John's churchyard in central Southend, his wife outliving him by over twenty years – a childless union.

An indication of this Southend author's popularity was his inclusion in the set of Famous British Authors cigarette cards issued in 1937 by WD&HO

Wills, alongside such luminaries as Hillaire Belloc and J.B. Priestley. Even John Betjeman was involved in the (unsuccessful) campaign to save Deeping's birthplace from demolition, saying 'I would be prepared to stake my literary reputation on acclaiming the excellence of the early work of Warwick Deeping'. To ensure that George Warwick Deeping is not forgotten, the Warwick Deeping Appreciation Society was set up in 2000.

Warwick Deeping. (Courtesy of W.D. & H.O. Wills)

Ian Dury

Pop Star

One of the original rockers, Ian Dury, an only child, was born in 1942 during the Blitz in Harrow, Middlesex. The family promptly moved out to his grandmother's safer haven in Mevagissey in Cornwall, and even spent some time in Montreux, Switzerland, where his dad, a bus driver, had found superior employment as a chauffeur. In 1946 his mother and father separated and Ian and his mother (a health visitor) went to live with an aunt in Cranham.

Ian was five when he started at Upminster infants' school but contracted polio around the same time – seemingly after swimming in a public pool at Southend-on-Sea. This was a common disease at the time, with 58,000 people affected between 1947 and 1958. Ian was left partially paralysed and he was sent to a special school in Sussex, with a tough regime. His mother cast round for an alternative, but her choice of the Royal Grammar School in Buckinghamshire was in some ways worse because it discouraged Ian's musical interests, with its emphasis on academia. Hence, he rebelled and became involved in an early skiffle group.

Ian Dury (left) and The Blockheads. (Author's Collection)

Luckily, one of the O-levels he achieved was in art, opening the way to the Walthamstow College of Art in East London with its bohemian students and life-style. This was where he met his first wife, Elizabeth (Betty), the daughter of two Welsh painters. They married in 1967 and had a daughter, Jemima, with a son, Baxter, born after a move to Buckinghamshire.

Although he had started writing songs while holding down a job as a lecturer, it was the formation of Kilburn and the High Roads, which became Ian Dury and the Blockheads, which was to lead to real success in twentieth-century popular culture. By the late '70s, he had acquired a reputation for memorable lyrics about such characters as 'Billericay Dickie' who managed a string of liaisons in the back of his Cortina with ladies from Shoeburyness to Burnham on Crouch (*'a seasoned-up hyena couldn't have been more obscener'*). Then there were such hits as 'Reasons to be Cheerful, Part Three' and 'Hit Me with your Rhythm Stick' – which sold a million copies in January 1979 alone.

As the music scene changed in the eighties, he tried his hand at acting and painting – to some acclaim. In 1998, however, he went back on the road, four years after his first wife had died of cancer and two years after he had been similarly diagnosed, with cancer of the colon. He knew that the cancer had spread to his liver and that his condition was terminal but, regardless, he had married the sculptress Sophie Tilson, the mother of his two youngest children.

On stage, he had been described as a 'spivvy update of a Dickensian villain' complete with the stick he needed for support. In fact, it seems that Ian Dury found it easier to cope with being stared at because of his limp than because he was famous. As a father himself, he had campaigned for disabled children, and his early death in March 2000 is best described as, to use his own words, 'What a Waste'. However, The Blockheads continue to perform, sometimes accompanied by Phill Jupitus, a Leigh-on-Sea resident.

Noel Edmonds

Television and Radio Presenter

Noel was born on 22 December (the clue's in the name) 1948 in Ilford, the only child of teachers Dudley and Lydia Edmonds. Primary school was the local Glade Primary in Clayhall. As a headmaster's son, it is perhaps not too surprising that he then gained a place at Brentwood Public School which resulted in a clutch of O- and A-levels. This meant he could study psychology, philosophy and sociology at Surrey University.

However, rather than pursue this degree, he developed an interest in pirate radio. This was the Swinging '60s when some of the pirate ships were moored off the Essex coast, and, while working as a disc jockey in local hospital radio (and at Ilford Palais), he sent off audition tapes to Radio Caroline and Radio London. One of these tapes was kept by Radio London disc jockey Tony Windsor after the pirate radio ships were closed down in 1967. Although this closure scuppered Noel's ambitions, resulting in his becoming a student teacher in Essex for a while, Tony Windsor became Programme Director of Radio Luxembourg the following year, and he was invited to an audition.

In November 1968, he started with Radio Luxembourg as a news reader, leading to work at Radio 1 and then Radio 2 as an announcer, promoting programmes and competitions. His next lucky break was the result of Kenny Everett having 'flu in February 1970, meaning Noel got the chance to take over the show, launching his radio broadcasting career to another level. His *Breakfast Show* attracted a record twelve million listeners when he took over from Tony Blackburn in 1973 – for ten years.

He moved into television as one of the presenters of *Top of the Pops*, followed by his own Saturday morning children's show *Multi-Coloured Swap Shop*, Noel's first long-running television programme which aired from 1976 to 1981. More importantly perhaps, he also proved popular with mainstream audiences, hosting *The Saturday Roadshow, Telly Addicts, Come Dancing* and *Top Gear. Noel's House Party* (1991-1999) introduced the public to Mr Blobby, and earned him some of his millions from merchandising spin-offs, even including three short-lived theme parks called Crinkley Bottom.

A few years in the media wilderness when he fell out with the BBC ended in Noel's divorce from his second wife (they had been living in Devon with their four daughters) and a developing interest in business, and, latterly, in cosmic ordering. He has been able to buy a hotel in Chippenham, an Aston Martin, a house in France and a helicopter to demonstrate his diverse interests and business acumen. You could say that this also proves that the decision not to follow his parents into teaching was the right one.

Noel's rebirth in the last few years as the presenter of *Deal or No Deal* has far exceeded Channel 4's expectations, although not necessarily his own. It has pulled in as many as four million viewers, and, if you watch carefully, demonstrates Noel's professional disdain for earpieces and autocues.

Noel Edmonds. (Author's Collection)

Lee Evans

Stand-up Comic and Actor

Although Lee was born in 1964 in Avonmouth (Bristol), his father was a travelling musician and comic, and the family moved around the country quite a bit. He and his brother seemed to grow up in digs, theatres and clubs sitting in the back of the car or spending time backstage talking to dancers while Dave Evans was on stage. Essex seemed to be a more popular port of call than most. Lee spent a number of years at Billericay (secondary) School. At least one of the homes the family lived in was on an Essex council estate.

Lee Evans. (Author's Collection)

They lived for a while in Wales when Lee was a teenager, and at one time he played drums in a punk band, winning a contest as a result. But he did try a few different outlets for his diverse talents – a spell at art school and a stint as a boxer – before following in his father's footsteps.

First and foremost, Lee had the ability to make people laugh. As a result, he spent six years touring clubs across the British Isles, and remembers The Joker at Southend-on-Sea, its earliest comedy club. After a regular spot at The Comedy Store in London, his big break was the Edinburgh Festival in 1993 when he won the Perrier Award – promptly followed by a breakdown, the sudden success proving too much. However, in the same year he managed to perform two sell-out nights at the London Palladium, and started his television appearances.

In 1995, Lee moved into films, including the successful *There's Something About Mary* and *Mousehunt*. He has appeared frequently on stage, including such diverse productions in the West End as Samuel Beckett's *Endgame* and Mel Brooks' *The Producers*. Yet, he regards stand-up as his 'thing' and acting as a 'hobby'.

His was the first comedy gig to be held at the splendid O$_2$ in London in 2007, and he broke his own record for staging the biggest ever live solo comedy act. In under an hour, 15,000 seats were sold. Not that Lee Evans is a stranger to breaking records: ten years earlier (1996) he broke all box office records for a solo comedian at a Stoll Moss Theatre when he managed a sell-out eight-week run at the Lyric Theatre in London. He was also the first solo comic to play Wembley Arena (2002), performing to 20,000 people. Record-breaking sales of his DVDs demonstrate the popularity of this energetic and very physical performer.

Lee has lived for a number of years in and around the Southend area with his wife Heather and daughter Molly. They married in 1981, when Lee was just seventeen. Their daughter was born in 1994, and their most recent move was in 2007 to Billericay. On the rare occasions when Lee is not working, the family spend weekends in Brighton, where Lee's writing partner lives.

Lynn Fontanne (1887–1983)

Actress

Not a familiar name in the twenty-first century, but half of one of the greatest husband-and-wife acting teams of twentieth-century theatre – along with husband Alfred Lunt. Lynn was born to a French father and Irish mother at Station Terrace, Snakes Lane, Woodford, in 1887; the house now a bookmakers.

Her father ran a printing business in Clerkenwell but it seems he was not as successful as he had hoped, so Lillie (her original name) and her three sisters were taken out of school early on to earn some money to assist the family fortunes. As Jules Fontanne was made bankrupt in 1895, this decision was understandable. Finances were quite a bone of contention in their Woodford home, and all four girls left home early on to escape the arguments.

Lillie had always wanted to be an actress, and had the wherewithal to present herself at the Chelsea home of Ellen Terry, the most famous actress of the period. Being tall and slim, Lillie was not in current fashion which favoured the petite and plump. However, Ellen Terry took on the twelve-year-old as a student, resulting in the Essex girl appearing on stage in 1905 in *Alice-sit-by-the-fire*, her debut. She was then introduced to the manager of the Drury Lane Theatre who cast her in *Cinderella*, and in 1910 she sailed to New York to appear in a play which ran for just three weeks.

Lynne Fontanne from the
Theatre Magazine, August 1923.
(Author's Collection)

During the First World War, Lillie had to take odd jobs such as modelling or as a chauffeuse when other parts were not forthcoming. In 1914, she had a major success in *Milestones*, and met American actress Laurette Taylor the same year. Two years later, Lillie went to America to appear on stage with Taylor. By 1918, she had met Alfred Lunt, a young actor, when backstage at the New Amsterdam Theatre.

The couple were married in 1922. Lynn, as she now was, resisted Hollywood offers, accepting parts in just three films between 1924 and 1943. There were some later television appearances, but the duo were renowned for their dedication to theatre, and enjoyed touring especially in remote areas where theatre was less common. Noel Coward became a personal friend; their sophisticated style ideal for his plays.

Their first UK appearance was in London in 1929 at the St James Theatre, in *Caprice*. Returning again in 1934, 1938 and 1942 onwards they became as well known in the UK as in the US. During the 1940s the partnership was as highly regarded as that of Ellen Terry and Henry Irving, and has only since been rivalled by that of Laurence Olivier and Vivien Leigh. Their last performance in England was in 1958 in a production of *The Visit*. As a team they appeared in twenty-six plays, the biggest hit being *O Mistress Mine* which ran for 451 performances in New York from January 1946 onwards, and then toured for three years, playing 400 venues.

A Swedish-style farmhouse called Ten Chimneys in Wisconsin (now a museum) was their permanent base, although they had an apartment in New York. Lynn received the gold medal of the American Academy of Arts and Letters in 1935, and in 1964 she and Alfred received the United States Freedom Medal, with a Tony to follow in 1970. They had pretty much retired by the 1960s and in 1977 Alfred died followed by Lynn in 1983, allowing a new generation of method actors to take over their considerable mantle. The couple did not have children, focusing instead on their careers – and their four dachshunds. A theatre was named after them in New York in 1958, the Lunt Fontanne, a considerable honour, and there was even a US postage stamp with their image in 1999.

Nearer home, a plaque was unveiled at Lynn Fontanne's Woodford Green birthplace in 2002 by Donald Sinden, a personal friend of the couple. He described Lynn as 'the most glamorous woman I had ever met'; a fitting memorial.

John Fowles

Writer

A plaque remains on the modest house where John Fowles was brought up – in Fillebrook Avenue, Blenheim Park, Leigh-on-Sea. He was born in 1926. His father, Robert, had trained as a solicitor, but had felt obliged to enter the family tobacco-shop business in London, commuting there every day in his bowler hat and suit. John's mother, Gladys, was a schoolteacher. Alleyn Court School in Southend was John's first school, where the Essex captain (Denys Wilcox) taught him cricket. Bedford School came next.

He acquired a reputation during his lifetime for criticising his dull background, its crassness and suburban nature. However, although he lived with his parents until the age of twenty-three, his own life was anything but dull. For the last year of the Second World War he attended Edinburgh University and then did eighteen months' military service in the Royal Marines. Finishing his education at New College Oxford, his prowess in German and French secured him firstly a teaching job at the University of Poitiers and then at Anargyrios College on Spetsai.

It was on this idyllic Greek island that he fell for Elizabeth, the wife of a fellow teacher. Two years later, back in London, Elizabeth left her husband and her daughter for John, in spite of his acknowledged affairs with a couple of his students. They married in 1954 and John taught at St Godric's College until 1963, writing in his spare time, with the usual rejections. Until, that is, *The Collector*, a mix of thriller and conflict, was published in 1963 – the sale of the film rights enabled him to give up the day job.

The success of *The Collector* helped John Fowles to sell the film rights to *The Magus* before he had finished it. The book was inspired by Shakespeare's *The Tempest* and illustrates John's interest in psychology. But, ironically, this film (starring Michael Caine) was less successful than the first (with Terence Stamp).

By this time, 1968, the couple were living in Dorset, although Elizabeth didn't like the county, especially in the winter, and John really wanted to live in France. Instead, they settled, after a couple of moves, for a large historic house with an enormous garden in Lyme Regis.

As John's muse, critic and editor, Elizabeth had an influence on his next success in 1969: *The French Lieutenant's Woman*. The option money for the film rights for this, and an advance for another novel, *Daniel Martin*, earned him half a million dollars in one week in 1977. He may not have written many novels (four between 1970 and 1990) but it seems he didn't need to.

Elizabeth died of cancer in 1990 shortly after diagnosis, and John, after a year of grieving, got involved with several much younger women. Eventually, however, in 1998, he married a family friend, Sarah Smith. He had his own health problems, including a stroke ten years earlier and heart surgery, and had become reclusive, but Sarah encouraged a return to his writing.

John Fowles. (Courtesy of Ian M. Cook)

Before his death in 2005, he had published a collection of essays (*Wormholes*) and his *Journals*, in two volumes.

Although he had no children of his own, John did stay in touch with his step-daughter, in spite of the unpromising start to their relationship. And, on the subject of family, it is interesting that his father had also written a novel, based on his First World War experiences, but it was never published. Despite John's scornful attitude towards his parents and his upbringing, he used fragments of Robert Fowles' battlefield descriptions in a passage of *The Magus*. A belated compliment? It would seem so.

Jimmy Greaves

Footballer

Jimmy was just six weeks old when, in 1940, his family moved from Manor Park, East London to Dagenham after a bombing raid. He, his parents, his brother Paul and his sister Marion, lived in Ivy House Road until 1950. In the '40s, the area was surrounded by open fields, and the house had a generous 300ft garden.

As treasurer of the Fanshaw Old Boys amateur football club, Jimmy's dad was given an old football no longer needed, and Jimmy's football-playing days began. His dad was promoted from railway guard to tube-train driver in 1950, and the family moved again to be nearer his work: to a newly-built council house in Huntsman Road, Hainault. He continued to travel to school in Dagenham – eight miles away – by bus. At Southampton Lane Juniors he played his first football game for the school team.

Jimmy Greaves. (Author's Collection)

At eleven, Jimmy's next school was Kingswood secondary school, Dagenham, and he again secured a place in the school football team. He became captain of the team, and head boy for the school. When not playing for the school on Saturday mornings, he loved the cinema; in Barkingside alone there were six to choose from.

In his final year at Kingswood, Jimmy had trials for both Essex and London Schoolboys, but was spotted by a Chelsea scout. He started as a gopher in Chelsea's club office while learning his trade, and was paid £3 per week plus £2 per week towards his accommodation expenses. After two years, and scoring 122 goals in the 1956-1957 season (a South East Counties league record), he was offered a full-time contract. He and his girlfriend, Irene, were delighted with his signing on fee: £50.

Irene became his wife when Jimmy was in his first season with Chelsea. They married in Romford Registry Office on a Wednesday, due to football commitments. They set up home in a flat in Wimbledon football ground, oddly within the main stand, a very appropriate setting. By 1958, Irene was pregnant.

Chelsea agreed to rent a club-owned bungalow in Great Nelmes Chase, Hornchurch, to Jimmy and Irene. It was a better place for their baby, Lynn, surrounded by green fields with a farm nearby (Lillyputts Farm).

Very soon, Jimmy had become the First Division's leading goal scorer and made his debut in international football in 1959. At home, he and Irene had had to deal with the death of their second baby, Jimmy, who contracted pneumonia at just four months. This loss was followed by another pregnancy, and the prospect of a move to Italy when he was approached by AC Milan. It sounded like the ideal new start, but he was unhappy from day one, and Tottenham paid Milan £99,999 for him just months later, a record at the time. Not that it was surprising given that, at twenty-one, Jimmy was the youngest player in English football history to have scored 100 League goals.

The family, including latest addition Mitzi, lived with Irene's parents in their council house on the Harold Hill Estate in Dagenham for a few months before buying their own house at No. 22 The Fairway, overlooking a common and a golf course. Son Danny was born in 1963 and Andrew in 1966. They moved again, to Hulton Moat, and then back to another house in The Fairway in 1970. The same year, he was, unexpectedly, sold off to West Ham. By this time, he was no longer enjoying his football and his publicised problems with alcohol led to a rift between him, his career and his wife. After they divorced, she moved to a smaller house in Upminster with the children, and Jimmy lived in a flat in Wanstead, until they re-married in 1979.

During his football career, Jimmy Greaves finished as leading goal-scorer in the First Division six times, scoring a record tally of 357, and scored on his debut for every senior team he played for. A survivor, Jimmy has re-invented himself in his post-football years – as television pundit, newspaper columnist, after-dinner speaker, and author. Oh, and he can name every pub between Aldgate East and Southend.

Sally Gunnell, OBE

Athlete

Sally, like her two older brothers, was born at the family farm at Chigwell, she in 1966. The 300-acres was an oasis of grassland and hills, with a dairy herd her father had brought from his previous farm, yet just a few miles from central London. The hay bales came in handy for early hurdling practice.

Both Les and Rosemary Gunnell, her parents, had been competitive athletes during their youth, and Les had run successfully at county level. Although Sally always thought of athletics as a hobby during her schooldays, she managed to fit a lot of sport into her days at Chigwell County Primary. She started taking sport a bit more seriously from the age of eleven, and was encouraged by her PE teacher to join Essex Ladies athletics club at Woodford as a 'minor' as she was too young to even be a 'junior'.

By the time Sally started at West Hatch secondary school, she was involved in sport during every break as well as before and after school, and joined every possible team. Although she was part of a championship netball team, athletics was always her favourite, the sport at which she excelled, and for which she received serious training at Essex Ladies. She started off with the long jump, and, when spotted by national coach Bruce Longden, moved on to the pentathlon and then to the heptathlon. The latter events meant that Sally had to learn how to hurdle, and much of her training then took place at Crystal Palace in South London. Once she focused on hurdling, she became number one in the world for women of her age (eighteen), and held the British Junior Record for the 100m hurdles (13.30 seconds).

Sally Gunnell. (Author's Collection)

After leaving school, Sally had to find jobs that allowed her time for training; she tried being a barmaid at a bar in High Beech at Epping, then a nanny, and then in 1986 secured a part-time office job at a London accountants. This was the year that she won her first gold for England at the Commonwealth Games (for the 100m hurdles), and she was able to use the local gym at lunchtimes, and get back to her training in the evenings. By the time Sally competed at the Seoul Olympics (in 1988), her employer had merged with a larger accountancy practice, and they were very flexible with regard to the time off she needed.

Sally's first overseas tour was to Australia and New Zealand in 1985. This is where she met Jon Bigg, a Brighton based athlete. They moved in together three years later, living in a Brighton flat for part of the week, travelling to different events and working at their day jobs for the rest of the week. It was a busy period, even without the Olympics when Sally set a British record for the 400m hurdles, although she missed out on the medals. Following success in the 1990 Commonwealth Games when Sally came home with two gold medals and a silver, and in the World Championships (a silver and a new British record for the 400m hurdles), her training for the Barcelona Olympics meant that she was down to working one day per week.

After her gold medal at Barcelona, even one day's work per week became impossible. But she will always be grateful to the company (Pannell Kerr Forster) for their sponsorship. Sally and Jon flew out to Florida to marry with fifty-two friends and family in attendance.

Sally maintained her number one title for a number of years, but started having Achilles tendon problems during 1996 and retired in 1997. She is the only woman to have held European, World, Commonwealth and Olympic 400 metre hurdles titles at the same time. She was awarded the OBE and was the subject of *This is Your Life*.

Today, the Essex golden girl is the mother of three boys (Finley, Luca and Marley). She works as a television presenter, is involved with a number of charities, and has written four books. Now settled in Brighton, Sally still visits her Essex roots.

Johnny Herbert

Racing Driver

Essex has produced a number of iconic racing drivers, but Johnny Herbert is probably the best known. He was born in Brentwood in 1964, and was brought up in Billericay and Brentwood. By the age of ten Johnny was already interested in racing, although at this stage he was racing in karts at Tilbury and at Buckmore Park (Kent). His parents, Bob and Jane, spent all their weekends supporting him. He was British junior karting champion in 1978 and British senior karting champion in 1979 and 1982 (135 cc).

As soon as he left school, he went to work selling spare parts for karts, and learning how to build them. The job was based in Kent, meaning a thirty mile cycle ride every day there and back from Johnny's home (which was then in Romford).

It was not surprising to his family that he built a successful career in motor racing. He moved up to Formula Ford in 1983, and won the prestigious Brands Hatch Formula Ford Festival title in 1985. He had won a Formula Three title by 1987, but was stopped in his tracks by a horrific crash at Brands Hatch in 1988. His feet were so badly injured that any future at all in motor-racing looked unlikely for a while.

But this setback did not end Johnny's career, only his reputation for being invincible. He won the Le Mans race in 1991, and was back on top form in 1995 with wins at Silverstone (his first Grand Prix win) and Monza (the Italian Grand Prix), and won the European Grand Prix in 1999, while driving for Benetton. His F1 career came to an end in 2000. It says a lot about him that so many drivers turned out for his farewell party which followed the Malaysian Grand Prix.

As recently as April 2008, the 'Romford Rocket' secured his first championship title since claiming the Le Mans Series laurels in 2004 when he triumphed in the final two races of the inaugural Speedcar Series in Dubai, clinching the championship crown.

Domestically, he is married to Becky with two daughters, Chloe and Amelia. In 1996, Johnny and his family moved to Monaco. Johnny's parents stayed in Essex, at Margaretting Tye.

Johnny Herbert.
(Photograph by David Cunliffe.
www.johnnyherbert.co.uk)

Sir Ian Holm, CBE

Actor

As a result of Ian's father's job – Medical Superintendent at Barley Lane Mental Hospital in Goodmayes, Ilford – Ian had rather an unusual start to life. Not only was he born there (in 1931), but he also spent a lot of time there as a child, although he was not in touch with any of the 'dangerous' patients.

The family lived in Ilford until the war years, which were spent uneventfully in Devon. Ian was at a boarding school for a time where he was bullied (his birth name, Ian Holm Cuthbert, didn't help) and subject to capital punishment prevalent in the school. The saddest wartime event for Ian was the death of his older brother Eric at the age of twenty-two, from cancer. After the war, Ian's parents moved to Worthing, and this time Ian was boarded – from 1946 to 1949 – at Chigwell Grammar.

It was at Worthing that he met provincial actor Henry Baynton. Ian had been interested in acting since seeing Charles Laughton in *Les Miserables* at the age of seven and Henry tutored Ian for his RADA audition. Having passed, somewhat to the surprise of his parents, he moved to relatives in Bromley, making the commute to college easier. His time there was interrupted by National Service and a nine month tour of America playing such parts as Peter Pan.

After RADA he was asked to join the RSC as the inevitable spear-carrier in *Othello,* with Anthony Quayle as the lead. He returned to Stratford in 1957 after a stint at Worthing Rep and on BBC Radio and became one of their long-term contract artists in 1961. Sadly, his father died in 1955 not having seen him on stage.

The 1960s also saw Ian on television (e.g. *The Wars of the Roses* directed by Peter Hall) and in film (e.g. *Oh! What a Lovely War* directed by Richard Attenborough). He won a BAFTA and a Tony during this decade for Best Supporting Actor roles, and was the *Evening Standard* Actor of the Year in 1965 for *Henry V* and *The Homecoming.* Although films took up a lot of his time in the '70s following a 1968 debut as Puck in *Midsummer Night's Dream*, he was still doing television, and theatre continued until 1976 when he had a series of panic attacks (interpreted by some as the onset of stage fright) when performing *The Iceman Cometh.* Since then, he has done little theatre, although he managed an acclaimed portrayal of *King Lear* at the National Theatre (1997) resulting in another *Evening Standard* Best Actor Award. There has not been a decade since Ian started acting when he has not won awards, and these have not diminished as he has grown older (six in 1998 for instance).

Off-screen, there has also hardly been a decade when he has not entered into a serious, if not marital, relationship. His first wife, Lynne, was an RSC wardrobe mistress and they had two daughters during their ten years together, divorcing in 1965. He then lived with a much younger wardrobe assistant,

Bee, after she fitted the diminutive actor with a club foot for *Richard III*. They had two children during their fourteen years together, but parted company in the late '70s before he moved in with photographer, Sophie. The birth of a son in 1980 was followed again by divorce a decade later. Ian married actress Penelope Wilton, but they split up after sixteen years, leaving him free to embark on yet another relationship – marrying artist Sophie de Stempel in Los Angeles in December 2003.

Ian has received recent acclaim for his role as Bilbo Baggins in the globally successful *Lord of the Rings* trilogy, but he has also had to fight off prostate cancer since taking on the role. He has been honoured with a CBE (1989) and a knighthood (1998) for 'services to drama'.

Now living in London, he can look back on a life and a career a world away from the sad place where he was born.

Ian Holm. (Author's Collection)

Sarah Kane

Playwright

Sarah Kane. (Iain Fisher)

Sarah was born in Brentwood Maternity Home in 1971. She was the only daughter and second child of a journalist and his wife, and was brought up in Kelvedon Hatch, attending Shenfield Comprehensive. Her parents were practising Christians, which explains some of her evangelical leanings as a teenager.

After acting with the Basildon youth theatre, she decided to study drama seriously and took up a place at the University of Bristol. Her preference moved from acting to directing, and she also wrote several short monologues which she performed at the Edinburgh Fringe in 1991 and 1992. University resulted in a first class honours degree, which she followed with an MA in playwriting at Birmingham University.

In 1994, she became literary associate at the Bush Fringe Theatre, and was by then living in Brixton. Her first full length play, *Blasted*, was staged at the Royal Court Theatre in 1995, and caused the biggest theatrical controversy of the decade. Raw, horrific and experimental, it received savagely hostile reviews, concentrating on its inclusion of masturbation, cannibalism, homosexual rape and defecation – a not too surprising reaction perhaps. The likes of Harold Pinter, however, sprang to her defence.

Her next plays were no less notorious – *Cleansed*, for instance, was set in a concentration camp (1998) and *Crave* was about obsessional love. She was a leading member of the In-Yer-Face theatre movement in London which shook traditional theatre up in the '90s, but she was also a lifetime depressive. Sarah was a woman of strong views: a vegetarian, anti-political correctness, and allegedly not interested in distinguishing between male and female lovers.

On several occasions, Sarah became a voluntary patient at London's Royal Maudsley Hospital. While recovering from a suicide attempt (at King's College Hospital), she hanged herself in 1999 – and the following year her play about suicidal depression, *4.48 Psychosis*, became her swan song at the Royal Court. A briefly flaring, but unforgettable, talent.

Ross Kemp

Actor

Although Essex-born members of the *EastEnders* cast over the years could fill a book in their own right, Ross Kemp is included here as the outstanding male representative. He was born in Barking in 1964, his mum a hairdresser, and his dad a policeman. It seems that dad, John Kemp, would have liked Ross to follow in his footsteps, but Ross was interested in acting from an early age, acting out sequences from *The Banana Splits Show* in the street.

His education was at Shenfield High School, where he excelled in sport; rugby was, and still is, a favourite. He went on to study drama at Southend College before securing a place at the Webber Douglas Academy in London. Fresh out of drama school, he was hired by the Palace Theatre's artistic director Chris Dunham in 1985, and it was there, in Westcliff-on-Sea, that he learned his craft. Ross's first role was as a pink munchkin in the *Wizard of Oz*, and the theatre's educational wing toured local schools, giving him plenty of experience.

Before his nine years in *EastEnders* as Grant Mitchell, Ross had appeared in *Emmerdale Farm* (now *Emmerdale*) from 1986-1987. He had also, ironically perhaps, played a policeman in *Birds of a Feather*, and, interestingly, a psychotic golfer (!) in a Kellogg's cereal advertisement. The Mitchell brothers made their debut in 1990.

Ross's move to ITV, post *EastEnders*, was for a reputed £1.2 million. He found himself in the position of being able to turn down £27,000 per week playing Buttons at the Hackney Empire to focus on more serious work. With ITV, Ross played a police officer and a lawyer respectively in *Without Motive* and *In Defence*. A bigger hit, ratings wise, was *Ultimate Force* in 2002.

His recent re-incarnation as documentary hardman on Sky One has served to distance Ross from his soap past. *Ross Kemp on Gangs* won the Bafta for best factual programme in 2007 and resulted in a book which sold some 80,000 copies. *Ross Kemp in Afghanistan* entailed his following the British Army's Royal Anglian Regiment during their deployment to Afghanistan in 2007 and, in preparation, Ross had to participate in military training. He is from their East Anglian recruiting area, and his father served with their predecessors (the Royal Norfolk Regiment). Working with Essex and East Anglian youth gave this programme an authenticity sometimes sadly lacking in such 'worthy' broadcasts.

At Christmas 2007, Ross did accept an offer of a pantomime, as, by then, he no doubt felt he had more than established his serious credentials. He played an evil henchman in *Snow White* at Wimbledon.

Away from television Ross has another interest (apart from rugby): poetry. Also not so well known is his ongoing link with his Essex roots via his involvement with the Woodland Trust to conserve woodland in the Fordham area, near Colchester. He married his long-time girlfriend, Rebekah Wade, the *Sun*'s editor, in Las Vegas in 2002, although they were alleged to be living in separate South London establishments early in 2008.

It is probably to his father that Ross owes his high-profile interest in politics. Ross is a vocal supporter of the Labour party. He also shares common ground with his brother, Darren, who is an award-winning documentary maker. Ross has of course not closed the door on Grant Mitchell, as Grant seems to be the main ammunition utilised by the BBC whenever *EastEnders* is overtaken by *Coronation Street* in the ratings wars. Listen out, too, for his distinctive voice-overs too numerous to mention.

Ross Kemp. (Author's Collection)

Kathy Kirby

Singer

Kathleen O'Rourke, born 20 October 1938 in Ilford, was the eldest of three children brought up by their Irish mother after their father left home when they were very young. Her schooling was at the Ursuline Convent School in Brentwood, and her singing voice meant a) that she became a member of the school choir, and b) that her mother was persuaded to find the money for her to have private singing lessons (from the age of nine).

Although Kathy's initial love was for opera, she soon diverted to a preference for pop music once a teenager. Having won numerous local singing competitions, she had enough confidence in her ability to approach the legendary '30s bandleader Bert Ambrose when he was appearing at Ilford's *Palais de Danse* in 1954. Ambrose was aware that there was talent under the trappings of dyed blonde hair, tight dress and stilettos. She added two years to her age, and he agreed to audition her, resulting in her first contract: £10 per week for a thirteen week tour.

That tour led to others, to support work for such singers as Cliff Richard, to cabaret and nightclub work, all the time improving her craft. With Ambrose's help, she even released two records (with Pye) before the age of twenty-one, but it wasn't until a television spot on *The Arthur Haynes Show* that she was offered regular work. She was spotted by the producers of *Stars and Garters*, which first aired in 1963, and became one of the main attractions of the series.

Switching to Decca, Kathy finally hit the pop charts with 'Dance On', followed by her biggest hit 'Secret Love', which became her 'theme' tune. It didn't make number one because it was competing with the Beatles and Cliff Richard.

Fame came with her success on records and on television – she was doing *Thank Your Lucky Stars*, *Ready Steady Go*, and even *Sunday Night at the London Palladium*. In fact, by early 1964 she had a thriving fan club, her talent being considerably assisted by her Hollywood-inspired glamour.

Surpassing this accolade, however, was the BBC's offer in 1964 of eighteen *Kathy Kirby Shows* at £1,000 per show, making her television's highest paid female star. On her shows, her guests included Tom Jones, Billy Fury, Buddy Greco and Jessie Matthews.

Another career highlight followed in 1967 when she was chosen to represent the UK in the Eurovision Song Contest, managing a respectable second place. Her income rocketed to such an extent that she could afford to live in Mayfair: she was averaging £60,000 p.a. by 1970, with Ambrose as her manager, and, as she revealed later, her lover. In spite of the power he held over her, it was a sad day in her life when she lost him in 1971, and she was chief mourner at his funeral.

Kathy began to make less happy headlines with frequent changes of agent, stormy relationships, and financial problems. She married a London policeman, Frederick Pye, in 1975, but, following a miscarriage, the marriage ended two years later at the same time as she was petitioned for bankruptcy. She sold her Brighton home, and her Barbican flat was re-possessed. Worse followed – outbreaks of violence (with police intervention), loss of control (resulting in medical intervention), and a lesbian lover (resulting in the latter's imprisonment for fraud). Life on stage, as she said herself, was easier for her than off.

Once the bankruptcy order was lifted, Kathy returned to performing, achieving success during her reliable times. Although she has turned down offers of work in recent years, her name and golden voice live on in many memories while she lives reclusively in South London. A biography was launched in 2005 and a musical, *Secret Love – What Really Happened to Kathy Kirby*, in 2008.

Kathy Kirby (Courtesy of Graham Smith. www.secretlove.info)

Penny Lancaster

Model and Photographer

Born in 1971 and brought up in Chelmsford, Penny is a classic example of what Essex can produce, and we should be proud of her. Bullied at school because she was skinnier and taller than her classmates, she has managed to turn these 'handicaps' into advantages. She may have hated her thirty-six inch legs at one time, but now they are her trademark.

After eight years at the Alma Rippon Stage School at Barkingside studying tap, modern and ballet, and passing exams at the Royal Academy of Dance, Penny started out as a fitness instructor, with a passion for aerobics. However, she was spotted by a scout who felt that she could have a more lucrative career in modelling which would make good use of her statuesque 6ft 1in height. Plenty of work in television commercials followed.

With an eye to her future, Penny moved on to studying photography at Barking College from 1998 to 2000 and took a BTEC National Diploma in Photography, passing with distinction. She actually met Rod Stewart at a Christmas party during her first year as a student. He invited her to take some photographs at a concert, and, after his split from wife Rachel Hunter, invited her out to dinner.

It is difficult to decide if her status as Rod Stewart's girlfriend helped her career. It certainly did her no harm: she was offered photographic assignments for *HELLO!* Magazine and became the face of Ultimo lingerie. Penny also brought out a best-selling fitness DVD. In 2005, she made her stage debut in *Tonight's The Night* (a musical about Rod Stewart) and she has appeared many times on television: with Neil Morrisey (in *Elixir Man*) and in such programmes as *Richard and Judy*, *Loose Women* and as co-presenter on *Birth Night Live*.

Seven years after their first meeting, Rod proposed atop the Eiffel Tower, when his divorce was pending. She was sporting her £20,000 engagement ring a few months later when she discovered she was pregnant, and they postponed wedding plans accordingly. Alastair Stewart was born in November 2005 (his seventh child but her first), and the couple married in June 2007 in Portofino on the Italian Riviera.

2007 was quite a year for Penny overall. She started by photographing numerous celebrities with their pets for a sell-out PDSA calendar, she had her work featured at the Ariel photography exhibition, as well as continuing her modelling career. Then came *Strictly Come Dancing* which introduced Penny to the general public. She managed to survive in the competition until week six, accrediting herself as a dancer and as a personality rather than just a pair of legs. She also did well on *Who Wants to be a Millionaire?*, appearing with her dancing partner Ian Waite and raising £10,000 for one of her favoured charities, the Lowe Syndrome Trust. Penny and her husband support a number of other charities and they are ambassadors for the Prince's Trust and patrons of WellChild.

Penny and Rod spend a lot of their time in their Essex mansion near Epping, although they are both fond of the Miami lifestyle. So at least this is one girl who hasn't strayed too far from her roots just yet.

Penny Lancaster. (Author's Collection)

Denise Levertov

Poet

Born in Ilford in 1923, Denise Levertov had exotic parents: her Welsh mother (a teacher) was named Beatrice Spooner-Jones Levertoff, and her father, Paul Levertoff (the original spelling of her surname), was a Russian Hasidic Jew (son of the Rabbi of Moscow) who became an Anglican parson after converting to Christianity. She was educated at home in Mansfield Road, along with older sister Olga, and showed an interest in writing from the age of five. This is not so surprising given that her reading was focused on such greats as Conrad, Dickens and Tolstoy. Her mother's main interest was in the arts and in creative writing, poetry and mythology. At twelve, Denise sent some poems to T.S. Eliot who replied encouragingly. Her first published poem (in 1940) was *Listening to Distant Guns*.

During the Second World War she was a civilian nurse, and she met an American travel writer, Mitchell Goodman, in 1947, a year after publishing her first book, *The Double Image*. They married and she moved with him to the United States in 1948. After settling in New York, they had a son, Nickolai, but divorced some years later. By 1955, Denise was an American citizen but she carried memories of the rivers and gardens of Essex in later life, writing of 'romantic and beautiful Wanstead and Valentine's parks'.

Early poetic influences in America were William Carlos Williams and Robert Creeley of the Black Mountain group. She was prolific in her output, experimenting with form and language in the '50s, and editing *The Nation*'s poetry in the '60s. With the advent of American involvement in the Vietnam War, Denise felt it was part of her role as a poet to decry the injustices and suffering of the Vietnamese. Her 1971 book, *To Stay Alive*, was one such collection of anti-Vietnam War letters, journal entries and discussions. She also took part in anti-war rallies and joined the War Resister's League.

Probably her best-known book of poetry was *The Sorrow Dance* (1967) dealing with her feelings about the war and about the death of Olga. Later poetry moved away from political to religious themes. She explored more than just the meaning of life, she explored being an outsider and about experiencing God; in *Evening Train* (1992) she wrote about a mountain as a metaphor for life and God.

To pay the bills, Denise was poetry editor of *Mother Jones* from 1975 to 1978, and taught at universities throughout the USA. For eleven years from 1982 she held a full professorship at Stanford University and after retiring she travelled doing poetry readings in the USA and England. By 1990, she had become a Roman Catholic.

Denise Levertov, a force in poetry that Essex should not forget, died in Seattle from complications due to lymphoma in 1997. But she leaves behind over twenty books of poetry, plus prose works, essays, criticism and translations. In her lifetime, she was honoured with the Shelley Memorial

Denise Levertov, by Chris Felver.
(Courtesy Bloodaxe Books)

Award, the Robert Frost Medal, the Lannan Award, the Lenore Marshall Prize, and a Guggenheim Fellowship.

Her 1962 work, *Contemporary American Poetry*, included a poem entitled, perhaps incongruously, *A Map of the Western Part of the County of Essex in England*. This refers to Hainault, Clavering, Stapleford Abbotts, Woodford, and:

In Ilford High Road I saw the multitudes passing pale under
the light of flaring sundown, seven kings
in sombre starry robes gathered at Seven Kings …

Dominic Littlewood

Television Presenter

In some ways an Essex stereotype, Dominic Littlewood has always been a grafter. He was born in 1965 and was brought up with three siblings in a small semi in Westcliff-on-Sea. Ann, his mother, was a teacher, and his father, Michael, was in the Royal Navy, but they both earned extra money when they could to support their brood. Holidays were spent in a camper van.

Dominic had his first holiday job with a travelling fair when he was fourteen, and he hasn't stopped working since. After leaving St Thomas More's High School for Boys in Westcliff, young Dominic worked in the shipbuilding industry for a while. This was not particularly lucrative in the '80s, and Dominic moved into the new and used car business. It is unlikely that at that stage he could have envisaged that he would become a popular and recognised television personality.

Dominic Littlewood. (Courtesy of Dominic Littlewood)

The television work started after he taught a West Country vicar how to be a second-hand car dealer in one month for Channel 4's *Faking It*. From being a successful self-employed salesman, this television appearance led to offers flooding in, and he was soon able to give up the day job and focus on presenting such series as *To Buy or Not to Buy*, *Beat the Burglar* and *Wrong Car, Right Car*. Further work has included co-hosting *The One Show*, and fronting *How I Made My Property Fortune* and the daytime consumer programme *Don't Get Done, Get Dom*. One of his favourite jobs was filming a holiday programme which included a visit to Cape Town.

When he was twenty-four, Dominic broke his neck on holiday in Australia as a result of 'larking around' on the beach. A month later, surgery back home left him in a body brace, but he fought his way back to enjoying water skiing, sailing and jet skiing on the estuary and he has won the celebrity sprint for BBC's Comic Relief. Apart from presenting, Dominic has also written material for *Top Gear Magazine*, and the *Daily Telegraph*. More recently, he has also taken part in *Strictly Come Dancing*, being the fifth celebrity to be voted off, a respectable result.

Dominic's parents sadly both died in their sixties earlier this century, and he lives the life of a single man. The town-house he lived in in Chalkwell (Westcliff-on-Sea) was very much a bachelor pad with estuary views, but his television work means that he spends so much time in London, he is unlikely to remain in Essex much longer. It will be Essex's loss.

John Lloyd

Tennis Player

One of three tennis playing brothers from Leigh-on-Sea, John is the most well known, having been regarded by some as Britain's number one in the 1970s. He was born in 1954 and was brought up in Chalkwell. He attended Chalkwell Primary where his drawings even then often contained a tennis element. Less happily, perhaps, memories of his first week at Southend High School are of being caned as some kind of warning so that he did not follow in brother David's mischievous footsteps. It seems he was not a fan of school and his older sister, Anne, apparently helped him 'forge' sick notes so that he could play truant.

John's parents settled in Leigh-on-Sea after the Second World War, first in a flat, then in a semi at Woodfield Road. His father commuted daily to London to his import-export business, but the family's social life centred around Westcliff-on-

John Lloyd (right) and his brother David. (Author's Collection)

Sea tennis club. Dennis Lloyd was a coach, having himself reached Wimbledon qualifying standard, and John picked up his first racket at the club when aged six. Brothers David and Tony (the youngest) were also keen players.

Just before his eleventh birthday, John reached the final of the under-fourteen's championships at Exmouth, and from the age of thirteen he travelled to Wimbledon every weekend to train with John Barrett (ex Davis Cup captain). He excelled as a junior player, winning the British Under-16 Championship in 1970 and the Junior Covered Courts Championship two years later. He had managed to extricate himself from school at the age of fifteen to concentrate on tennis.

In 1982, John won his first prize money: £350 at the Dewar Cup on Teesside. He used the prize money to go to the US and widen his experience.

Older brother David later became John's doubles partner, their ranking reaching the top five. They were the first brothers for seventy years to represent Britain in the Davis Cup (in 1976).

In 1977, John reached the final of the Benson and Hedges Championship in London and the final of the Australian Open, losing the Open in five sets to Vitas Gerulaitis. He was the last Brit to reach the final of a Men's Grandslam, and reached the semi-final of the Men's Doubles at Wimbledon in 1973 (with David). He also won the Wimbledon Mixed Doubles with Wendy Turnbull in 1983.

As an attractive blond bachelor, he was nicknamed Legs by the press. American Chris Evert – another Wimbledon legend – did not seem deterred by this attention, and they married in 1979 in a romantic candlelit ceremony at St Anthony's Church in Fort Lauderdale, Florida. The 100 guests included friends and family from John's home town in Essex.

The stresses of their professional lives were partly responsible for the divorce which followed eight years later. John had by then retired from professional tennis (in 1984) and was focusing on coaching.

Nowadays, John is often seen, and heard, as a tennis commentator for the BBC, especially around the Wimbledon season. More importantly, perhaps, he was delighted to take on the role of the Great Britain Davis Cup captain which he will hold until 2011. He lives in Los Angeles with second wife Deborah and teenage children Aiden and Hayley.

Victor Maddern

Actor

Victor Maddern's face will be recognised by everyone who has ever seen an English film from the 1950s and '60s, because he seemed to be in most of them, as well as appearing in such popular television series as *The Avengers*, *The Saint*, and *Dixon of Dock Green*. His name is not as well known as his face, as he was a character actor rather than a leading man.

Born in 1926 in St Albans Road, Seven Kings, Victor went to local schools William Torbitt primary and Beal secondary modern school before serving

Victor Maddern. (Author's Collection)

in the Merchant Navy during the Second World War. By the time he was medically discharged (1946), he had developed an interest in acting, which seemed much better than the alternative working options open to him once the war was over. Instead, he secured a place at the Royal Academy of Dramatic Art, not an easy task.

As an actor, he played a lot of servicemen, privates, sergeants, corporals, and was often cast in wide-boy or Cockney roles. His first film was as a trigger-happy soldier in *Seven Days to Noon* (1950) and he was credited with another 100 film roles (thirty-seven of them in the '50s alone) and probably another 100 uncredited. Comedy became a more prominent part of his work in the '60s with roles in several of the *Carry On* films, but his range was diverse – he turns up, for instance, as the Junkman in *Chitty Chitty Bang Bang* (1968).

He was just as busy with television work, taking on the role of Fruity Pears in *The Darling Buds of May* as late as 1992. His co-stars have included all the greats from David Niven to Sir John Mills. On stage, he, along with most British stage actors, made several appearances in the record-breaking West End production of *The Mousetrap*.

In the 1980s, Victor, a life-long Conservative, hit the headlines when he spoke out against the growing trend of explicit sex and swearing on television. During this period, he turned down a lot of work because he disapproved of the scripts, even if he was not called upon to do any swearing himself. He campaigned – unsuccessfully – for a new television channel with clean family entertainment.

Essex was the place that Victor chose to make his home with wife Joan, with a house and farm in the North Ockendon area (which, incidentally, he was willing to hire out on occasion as a location, e.g. for the television series *Softly, Softly* in the late 1960s). The couple had four daughters.

In 1993, he died in St Joseph's Hospice in East London after a short illness (probably a brain tumour). However, his funeral was held at Leigh-on-Sea, near to where one or two of his daughters lived, and he was cremated at Southend crematorium. His unexpected death becomes more tragic as the years go by, as he was not a fan of the celebrity circuit and did not have what is now regarded as part of the job, i.e. an inclination to write it all down. What a lot of fascinating stories he could have told…

Richard Madeley

Television Presenter

Richard was born in Romford in 1956, but early on in his childhood the family moved to Hartswood Road, Brentwood, opposite a wood, giving Richard a taste of the countryside. On his birthdays, treats included a picnic in Epping Forest, although a trip to London was another favourite. His sister, Liz, is four years older, and was born when their parents lived in Ontario (their mother is Canadian, although their father is British). It seems the three of them moved back here to take advantage of the NHS.

The local junior school at Rush Green, Romford, was Richard's first experience of education, and on passing his eleven plus he moved on to Coopers' Company School in Bow, East London. He was, with other Essex boys, an outsider, commuting by train to and from school. As a result, he became the victim of bullying at Coopers' and when Richard eventually confronted his father about his concerns he was moved to Shenfield Tech, a co-ed.

Initially, Richard tried to join the RAF as a fighter pilot, but was turned down due to being slightly short-sighted and under par at maths. His second choice of career was reporting, which was inspired by his father's memories of being a journalist in the UK and Canada. Although the plan was to read English at university, he was unexpectedly offered a job as a cub reporter at the *Brentwood Argus* when he applied for work experience. Starting with writing up weddings and funerals, he progressed to reporting for the *East London Advertiser* and, around the same time, he moved into a flat in Leytonstone, East London. Rather than the more predictable move to Fleet Street, Richard started applying for jobs in local radio thanks to a suggestion from a colleague. BBC Radio Carlisle came up with an offer, and Richard set off up north.

The Carlisle bedsit was a bit lonely, and Richard entered into an early relationship with the girl in the downstairs flat, which quickly led to marriage, in 1977. Their honeymoon (on a caravan site in Somerset) was interrupted by a telephone call from Richard's mother with the devastating news that his father had died of a heart attack. He was just forty-nine.

Professionally, Richard moved on to reporting for Border Television, then Yorkshire Television, then Granada. He and Lynda, his wife, moved from their Carlisle house to Aberford. On day one at Granada in 1982, he met Judy Finnigan. Both were experiencing marital problems and eventually the inevitable happened: they moved in together, and had a son, Jack, (regarded as something of a miracle after two earlier miscarriages) just five months before both divorces came through. Manchester Registry Office was the venue for their quiet wedding. Daughter Chloe came along soon after, with less drama than had been attached to Jack's longed-for birth.

At Granada, their pairing in *This Morning* from 1988 was the start of their success story as the most in-demand two-some on television. The programme headed south when it became an issue getting guests to the Manchester studios, and the family moved to Hampstead. By the year 2000, they were able to afford a holiday home in Talland Bay, Cornwall.

Channel 4's idea for a tea-time slot in 2001 was a new challenge for Richard and Judy, and another huge ratings success until they decided to call it a day, the last series due to air in 2008. During their time there, they became the broadcaster's highest earners. Future projects include writing books and fronting a new talk-show for a digital channel. Richard may have put his foot in it once too often, and may be too frank for some, but the couple have a justifiable claim as King and Queen of UK television.

Richard Madeley (and Judy). (Author's Collection)

Helen Mirren

Actress

Helen's grandfather, a Russian aristocrat and member of the Tsarist Army, arrived in Essex when her father was two. It seems he had been negotiating an arms deal in England and found himself stranded here, along with his family, after the Russian Revolution.

Helen's mother came from a family of butchers, and her father had fought Mosley's Black Shirts in the East End. The two of them worked together in a fabrics shop in Ilford, Essex. Helen, christened Ilynea Lydia Moronoff, was born in 1945 and her younger brother followed shortly afterwards. Their father, who'd also worked as a cab driver, felt obliged to look for more secure employment in order to provide for his new family, and ended up as the chief driving examiner at the Southend Test Centre.

As a result, the family moved to Satanita Road, Westcliff-on-Sea, when Helen was about two. Her first school, Hamlet Court Road Junior in Westcliff, is now a car park. Helen's earliest introduction to theatre was a visit to a show at the end of Southend Pier starring Terry Scott, which she absolutely loved. Her next experience was a little different: an amateur production of *Hamlet* by the Southend Shakespeare Society.

This in part decided her on a stage career, and, at St Bernard's High School in Westcliff, Helen excelled in Shakespearean studies, before proceeding to drama college. After winning a prize at the National Youth Theatre, she made quite an impression as the eponymous queen in *Antony and Cleopatra* despite her youth. From there came the RSC and her first film, *Herostratus*, in 1967. By 1970, she was a big name, but she often returned to the Southend area, to her old school or to visit her family. She still turns up occasionally, to sign her autobiography, perhaps, or to lend her support to the Palace Theatre in Westcliff-on-Sea.

Helen has appeared naked more often than any mainstream actress of her generation – for her 50th birthday she appeared 'tastefully' naked on the cover of the *Radio Times*. It is her lack of professional inhibitions that singled her out from the crowd, but it is her talent that keeps her going when her peers have disappeared into obscurity. There are few acting careers so diverse and so successful: from *Calendar Girls* to *The Madness of King George*, from the popular television series *Prime Suspect* to *The Queen*.

Successes include winning the Golden Globe in 1997, two Emmys in 1996 and 1999, three BAFTAs in 1992, 1993 and 1994, the Screen Actors Guild in 2002, the New York Film Critics Circle Award in 2001, the London Film Critics Circle in 2002 and Best Actress Awards at the Cannes Film Festival in 1984 and 1995, and another Golden Globe and Academy Award for best actress for *The Queen* in 2006.

Off screen, Helen certainly didn't rush into marriage. After earlier liaisons with James Wedge (a fashion photographer), Liam Neeson and Nicol

Williamson, she finally married American producer-director Taylor Hackford in 1997. They had been together for ten years by then. Children were never on the cards as Helen admits to not being a maternal type.

In her limited spare time, she campaigns actively for Oxfam against the small arms trade and for Action Aid.

Helen's career has offered her opportunities to travel all over the world, and she is truly Essex girl turned global superstar. Accorded the title of Dame of the British Empire in 2003 and a Doctor of the University of Essex in 2004, it is good to see her work and her background recognised.

Helen Mirren. (Author's Collection)

Bobby Moore, OBE

Football Player

Robert Frederick Chelsea Moore was born in Waverly Gardens, Barking in 1941, the only child for Robert and Doris. He went to Westbury School, and began playing football on Saturday mornings for the South Park Boys, part of the Ilford league. His first honour was the captaincy of Barking Primary School's football team, winning the Crisp Shield. Progress came as part of the Leyton Schools' team (he was attending Tom Hood High School in Leyton then) and the Essex Boys' team. A local scout spotted him and invited him to attend West Ham's youth intake.

While playing for West Ham's Metropolitan League side, Bobby debuted for England Youth in 1957 in a game against Holland. His debut for West Ham (v. Manchester United) was in 1958 to replace the tuberculosis-stricken Malcolm Allison. He became a West Ham regular and first played for England in 1962, making it into the World Cup Squad that year, and awarded the captaincy a year later by Alf Ramsey. 1962, incidentally, had an additional significance – it was the year he married Ilford girl, Tina, the girl he had met at Ilford Palais. Ilford was their choice for their first home together.

Bobby became the youngest ever winner of Footballer of the Year at the age of twenty-three. More success followed: the Hammers won the 1964 FA Cup and the 1965 European Cup Winners' Cup. Such successes however pale into insignificance compared with England's legendary performance in the 1966 World Cup Final when they famously beat West Germany 4-2, with Bobby as the proud captain. The memory of the blonde bombshell from Essex wiping his hands before accepting the World Cup trophy from the Queen is ingrained in every Englishman's psyche, football fan or no. Alf Ramsey was quoted as saying: 'Without him, England would never have won'. Not surprisingly, Bobby received an OBE in 1967.

On the home front, Bobby and Tina had two children (Roberta, born in 1965 and Dean in 1968) and moved a few miles to up-market Chigwell. As the family grew, so did the pressures of fame, although the marriage held fast for twenty-one years.

Bobby left West Ham in 1974, playing for Fulham and then trying American teams. After 1,000 matches, he finally retired as a player in 1978. He had represented England in 108 internationals, winning the majority of those he captained (57 of 90).

He joined Southend United in 1984 as Chief Executive and manager, following a short stint with Oxford City, but this too was short-lived. Southend were in the third division and having financial problems which went beyond relegation, and Bobby had trouble handling such a difficult situation, so chose to concentrate on burgeoning media work, football reporting and on promoting the Bobby Moore Soccer Schools.

When Bobby and Tina finally separated, he settled down with airline stewardess, Stephanie, in Leigh-on-Sea, but they moved to London when the Southend job came to an end. They married in December 1991, shortly after Bobby had been diagnosed with terminal cancer, which started in the colon but spread to the liver. He died in 1993, just a year after cancer had also taken his mother. He had been commentating on England v. San Marino at Wembley just a week before he died.

The most recent memorial to Bobby Moore is the statue at the entrance to the newly built Wembley stadium; an appropriate spot for this Essex champion.

Bobby Moore. (The David Goody Collection)

Dudley Moore, CBE

Actor and Comedian

From Dagenham schoolboy to Hollywood, Dudley Moore is the epitome of an Essex success story. His start in life was not exactly promising – he was born in 1935, the second child of 'Jock' (a railway electrician) and Ada, who were living on the Becontree housing estate in Dagenham. Another potential disadvantage was being born with his feet turned inwards (club feet) and with the left leg small and mis-shapen. Dudley's first operation was at two weeks old, and was followed by countless others in an attempt to correct his disability.

His musical mother, Ada, a Christian scientist, is said to have felt a combination of guilt and depression regarding her only son's defect, but nevertheless she encouraged his interest in music. This, of course, secured his future. Dudley's early piano lessons led to proficiency with the organ by the age of eight.

Before that, in 1939, the Moores had been evacuated to Plumstead in Norfolk, but were allowed back to Dagenham a year later where Dudley attended Fanshawe infants' school. Their home was promptly destroyed by a random bomb, and the family were moved again to another council house in Baron Road, identical to the first. Dudley lived there for the next eighteen years.

At the age of eleven, he won a scholarship to the Guildhall School of Music, and on Saturday mornings he studied harpsichord, violin, musical theory and composition as well as the organ. During the week he attended Dagenham County High School. The bullying and name-calling Dudley was subjected to – Hopalong Cassidy was a favourite – was dealt with by clowning around. It certainly did not affect his musical prowess, as he won a music scholarship to Oxford at nineteen, although he had to use a specially made boot with a two-inch platform to reach the organ pedals.

Before leaving university, Dudley had become an all-round entertainer – as jazz musician, revue participant, composer and actor for the drama school plays. After graduating, he toured as a jazz pianist and formed the Dudley Moore Trio, before teaming up with Peter Cook for *Beyond the Fringe* at Edinburgh, transferring quickly to London. The duo became household names with the BBC's *Not Only ... But Also* between 1965 and 1970.

Although he made a number of films with Peter Cook, Dudley also started solo starring roles with *30 is a Dangerous Age Cynthia*, marrying his co-star Suzy Kendall in 1968. His marriages did not last, Suzy being followed by actress Tuesday Weld in 1975; they met when he was in New York with *Behind the Fridge*, another Pete-Dud two-hander. They had separated by 1978, and Dudley settled in Los Angeles. His second Hollywood film *10* was a big hit, with *Arthur* in 1980 even bigger.

Dudley married actress Brogan Lane in 1987, followed in 1994 by Nicole Rothschild, the latter union resulting in accusations of assault and another divorce. He began to acquire a professional reputation for unreliability.

Perhaps he was displaying symptoms of the disease that was to claim his life – progressive supranuclear palsy.

This very special Essex boy received a CBE for services to entertainment just four months before his death in March 2002. Two sons, Patrick and Nicholas, and his older sister Barbara Stevens survived him. George Melly once said that 'It falls to very few to be truly original in jazz and to even fewer English people, and even fewer who come from Dagenham'. But he wasn't just a jazz musician, he could play Brahms, make you laugh (who could forget him as, ironically, the one-legged wannabe Tarzan?) and act his little cotton socks off. In fact, when John Gielgud (his *Arthur* co-star) died in 2000, one newspaper headlined his death as 'Dudley Moore's Butler dies'. Says it all.

Dudley Moore. (Author's Collection)

Andrew Motion

Poet

Born in Westminster Hospital in 1952, Andrew spent the first couple of years in a converted mill in Kimpton, a village in Hertfordshire. His mother it seemed felt it would be useful for London to be his place of birth on his passport in case he went 'globe-trotting' when he was older… In fact, he was very nearly born in a lift, as that is when his head appeared en route to the delivery room.

Andrew Motion.
(Photograph by Antonio Olmos.
www.andrewmotion.co.uk)

The family had moved to Essex before his brother Kit was born in 1955. Andrew's father worked in a London brewery, and they could by then afford a bigger place, plus the stream on the premises was not ideal with a baby and a toddler around. They settled on Little Brewers on the edge of Hatfield Heath, a straggle of houses around a common. His father had fond memories of Essex and of his time in the Essex Yeomanry preparing for the invasion of Normandy.

Andrew's primary school, The Barn, was eight miles away in Much Hadham, a village in Hertfordshire. At age seven, he was sent to boarding school: Maidwell Hall in Northamptonshire. According to his autobiography, this was not a particularly happy experience.

At home, the family were great fans of hunting, and most of the books in the house were about horses or hounds. By the age of nine, Andrew had his own pony, Tommy. At about the same time that Andrew moved on to Radley College, Oxford, his parents had found an old rectory at Stisted, near Braintree, never having really felt at home in Hatfield Heath. As the rectory's neglected interior took shape, Andrew was being introduced to poetry by Mr Way, the English tutor. Thomas Hardy became a particular influence at this stage.

It was just after his O-levels that Andrew developed contro malacia patella, making his knee joints ache frequently, and he ended up in The London Clinic for essential surgery. He quite enjoyed being housebound, with time to read poetry. Soon after, however, his mother was in a riding accident, and was in a coma for several years, dying when he was in his twenties. The experience makes its presence felt in much of his work:

*On this day in each year
no signposts point anywhere
but east into Essex,
and so to your ward*
                    from *Anniversaries*

Andrew read English at Oxford, gaining a first; and had his earliest volume of poetry published when he was twenty-four, and a lecturer at Hull University. A number of his poems refer to his childhood, particularly the woodland walks leading down to the River Blackwater.

As well as further anthologies, he is a renowned editor and biographer, acclaimed for his work on Keats and Larkin. In 1999 he was appointed Poet Laureate following in the footsteps of such notables as Wordsworth, Tennyson, John Betjeman and Ted Hughes. Since 2003 he has been professor of creative writing at Royal Holloway University, having spent over a decade in a similar role at East Anglia University.

The prizes he has won over the years demonstrate the standard of his work and the reputation he has acquired: the Newdigate Prize, the John Llewellyn Rhys Prize, the Dylan Thomas Award and the Eric Gregory Award. He has written poems about public events such as the Paddington rail crash and the death of Princess Diana. The media does not seem to phase him, and he has taken on somewhat of an ambassadorial role.

His father, remarried, continues living in Essex, but Andrew has settled in London with his second wife. He has two sons and a daughter.

Peggy Mount, OBE

Actress

Margaret Rose Mount, nicknamed Peggy, was born in East Street, Leigh-on-Sea in 1916. Her first school is now called Leigh Infants' School, in North Street. Although her grandfather was 'in entertainment' (he ran seafront entertainments), her father ran a nearby grocer's shop but he was not a well man and died when she was just fourteen.

As a child she enjoyed going out on the cockle boats, and was able to recall the *Endeavour* in particular. It was apparently through the Leigh Wesleyan Chapel that she became interested in acting, and acquired a voice coach/drama teacher. Her older sister (Nancy), who was a brilliant pianist, also went on to an acting career.

However, financial constraints prompted Peggy to train as a shorthand-typist to boost the family coffers. Thriftily, she managed to put aside coppers to buy 'late doors' tickets at local theatres, only available five minutes before

Peggy Mount. (Photograph by Eric Gray, Author's Collection)

curtain-up, and, occasionally, even managed to treat herself to a London stage production, securing her interest in the profession – which she did not regard as open to one of her unconventional appearance. It did not put her off joining in local amateur dramatics however.

It wasn't until 1944 that she managed to secure her first 'real' acting job, with Harry Hanson's Players, who had appeared in Southend when Peggy was in an amateur production which at least one member of the company fortunately went to see. She stayed with the Players for three years, and then took on the stage role of the raucous Emma Hornet in *Sailor Beware* at Worthing, but she was turned down initially for the West End run. When she was finally offered the role, she took the production to a three year run at the Strand Theatre, London, and eventually to a successful film (1956), although film was never her main focus, in spite of those she made in the 1960s, for example Mrs Bumble in *Oliver!*

Television, as is its habit, made her a household name in the late 1950s when she took on another battle-axe role, Ada Larkin in *The Larkins*, for ITV. Less well known were her classical roles – the nurse in Franco Zeffirelli's production of *Romeo and Juliet* at the Old Vic in 1960 for instance. Not to mention her Mrs Malaprop in Sheridan's *The Rivals*, and her perfectly Brechtian *Mother Courage*. Television work continued right through to the 1990s, including parts in *Inspector Morse* and *Casualty*, and she was an esteemed member of the Royal Shakespeare Company from 1983 to 1985.

Her private life was just that: private, and anonymous. She liked gardening and cooking, and preferred close relationships to marriage. Most of her friends were not from the showbiz world, and she enjoyed sailing off Foulness in her sailing boat, named, unsurprisingly, *The Dragon*.

The OBE she received in 1996 was better late than never, and Peggy carried on working until her sight failed her completely during a performance of Chekhov's *Uncle Vanya* in 1998. A stroke enforced a move from her Islington home to spend her last years in an actors' nursing home in Northwood, near London, and she died there in 2001. But Ma Larkin lives on.

(Genevieve) Alison (Jane) Moyet

Pop Singer-Songwriter

Alison's parentage (Anglo-French) is rather more exotic than her birthplace (Billericay). Her father was from peasant stock, allegedly a communist, and material aspirations do not seem to have featured in Alison's life. Alison was born in 1961 and was educated at Janet Duke County Junior in Basildon and Nicholas Comprehensive in Laindon, at which places she met up with future members of Depeche Mode. She admits to taking magic mushrooms, and, as a punk, found she had to dodge skinhead gangs. That voice survived it all.

Alison Moyet. (Courtesy of Haseeb Kayani)

When Alison left school at sixteen, she began a music foundation course at Southend College of Technology, but quit when she failed the theory and worked instead in a music shop. More studies followed in London – musical instrument technology this time, meaning she became a proficient piano tuner. In the meantime, she was able to sing in pub gigs in the Essex area.

Her first punk band was the Vandals, her next – more of a blues band – was The Screaming Abdabs. Then came backing vocals for The Little Roosters, but, more successfully, Yazoo followed in 1981. She 'found' Vince Clarke from an advertisement in *Melody Maker*, although she knew him from Depeche Mode. Their first single 'Only You' reached number two, and their first album *Upstairs at Eric's* went platinum in 1982. After their second successful album, Vince went on to form Erasure, and Alison began her solo career.

This was obviously the right decision as her debut album *Alf* shot to number one in the charts in 1984 and, after two years, reached quadruple platinum. Alison won the Brit award for Best British Female Solo Artist in 1985 and 1988, and she was one of the contributors to the Live Aid concert in 1986.

Her style changed for *Hoodoo* in 1991 and *Essex* in 1994, with a struggle going on between Alison's ideas and Sony's. This resulted in a long absence from recording. However, Alison proved she had more than one talent up her ever-growing sleeve, and she emerged in 2001 as Mama Morton in *Chicago* at London's Adelphi, stealing the show with her performances over six months.

Musical theatre does not seem to be her first love, however, and she released *Hometime* in 2002 with Sanctuary Records, securing yet another Brit nomination, and *Voice* in 2004 showing her diverse range. In the meantime, she also managed to do some narrating for radio. By 2005, she was back on stage, and on tour, with Dawn French in *Smaller*, a production for which she wrote several songs.

After twenty-five years as a singer, Alison Moyet's 2007 album *The Turn* entered the UK album charts at no. 21 and every date on her 2008 tour sold out in advance. Additionally, Yazoo Reconnected are all set to play a reunion tour, the first time Alison and Vince Clarke have performed live together since the 1980s.

This is one Essex girl who has kept her private life pretty private. She was first married to Malcolm Lee (a hairdresser), but they divorced after having a son (Joe). She had a daughter, Alex, after a relationship with her tour manager, and then married David Ballard, a support worker. The couple have a daughter, Caitlin.

More openly, Alison continues to be a supporter of Southend United football club. You can take the girl out of Essex, but you can't …

David Nixon

Magician

David Porter Nixon was born in December 1919 in North London, but his father, a lawyer whose hobby was magic, moved the family to Westcliff-on-Sea in 1922. He was the youngest of three children and enjoyed accompanying his father to the theatre to see the magic acts of the day, such as Maskelyne and Devant, who were pioneers of magic and cinematography. A present of a magic set one Christmas was the final prompt that saw David's interest in magic blossom. London's Gamages store became a favourite place to spend his pocket money, because it had a conjuring department.

At Westcliff High School, he was regarded as quick witted but with an element of reserve, an unexpected description of a future stage and television performer. An early local memory was of seeing *Twinkle*, a review that became a regular Wednesday matinée at the Shorefield Pavilion.

David Nixon (centre). (Courtesy of Steve Short)

By the time he left school, David and his tricks were already in demand at parties, and he joined the Magic Circle in 1937. He joined the Entertainments National Services Association at the start of the Second World War (pneumonia as a teenager prevented him from undertaking more active service), following an audition at the Theatre Royal, Drury Lane. Five years touring with ENSA turned David into a professional performer. In 1947, the first ENSA magician to perform on a submarine (!) was awarded with Associate Membership of the Inner Magic Circle with Silver Star for his work. A year later, he was using a stooge in his act, but not just any stooge: his name was Norman Wisdom.

The 1950s saw him moving on from summer seasons to television work, and an appearance in a show called *Garrison Theatre* (used for talent spotting) led to him being asked to replace a member of the *What's My Line* panel at very short notice. He was appearing at the same time in the London *Fol-de-Rols* concerts, and at The Windmill Theatre.

David's first wife, Margaret, a singer, died in 1952, only three years after they had wed. Ironically, this period was the start of his success. Apart from becoming a regular on *What's My Line*, and *Hello Playmates* (BBC radio), live appearances at such venues as the Savoy, and star billing at the Magic Circle's Annual Shows, he also had his own television series – *It's Magic* – followed by *Home and Dry*, appearing with his second wife, Paula. They had married in 1952, but this marriage was also sadly short-lived. They settled in South London and had a son, Nicholas, in 1955, but Paula died in a car accident just a year later, on her way to join David at their Christmas panto in Oxford.

Picking himself up, David continued in pantomimes and with television and stage work, culminating in his first Royal Variety Performance in 1958 – his next was in 1978. In between, he re-married, this time to Vivienne, a *Cordon Bleu* cook. They had a daughter, Amanda.

The last two decades of David's life were busy ones. He was never out of work and became a household name for anyone in Britain with a television set. He introduced Basil Brush to the television screen and hosted five runs of *Candid Camera*. In 1976, David achieved the honour of being elected King Rat of the Grand Order of Water Rats (the showbiz charity).

A heavy smoker, David was diagnosed with cancer in 1976, which at one stage he thought he had conquered. It was not to be, and his health finally failed him a few weeks before his fifty-ninth birthday. His December funeral, at the South London Crematorium, was attended by hundreds from showbiz and from charities. A little bit of magic lost from Essex – and the rest of the world.

Dermot O'Leary

Television Presenter

Although both parents were born and raised in Ireland, Dermot (or, rather, Sean Dermot Finton O'Leary) was born in Colchester in 1973. The family spent their summers in Wexford, Ireland, until Dermot was eleven and Dermot's Irish roots are also apparent from his Catholic education, at St Benedict's in Colchester. He was an altar boy at a Coggeshall Church – and he has an Irish passport.

Dermot O'Leary. (Author's Collection)

There were a lot of American airbases around the area where he was brought up, and he has reflected that he was a 'very good' American football player and played for the Gladiators from the age of fifteen until his mid-twenties. He was also interested in rugby, but nowadays he holds an Arsenal season ticket.

Dermot studied Media and Politics at Middlesex University, achieving a BA in Media and Television, and a minor in Politics. He started his career as a DJ on Radio Essex while writing letters to hundreds of production companies, finally being accepted as a runner, then a researcher, and finally a presenter on T4. While other presenting jobs followed, it was probably his work on *Big Brother's Little Brother* for Channel 4 that started to get him public recognition. Other Big Brother projects have included *Big Brain* and *Celebrity Hijack*, and he became even more well known when presenting the National Lottery's *1 vs 100* on BBC1 in 2006, followed closely by ITV's *The X Factor* in 2007.

Life without Big Brother (he quit in 2008) is just as busy for Dermot. He presents his own music show on BBC's Radio 2, runs his own production company – punningly called Murfia – and has future commitments to *X Factor* as well as doing one-offs such as ITV's *Extinct*.

Apart from his professional life, Dermot is actively involved in campaigning for the Catholic Development Agency (Cafod) – winning £32,000 for them on *Who Wants to be a Millionaire?* – and Everyman's Action Against Male Cancer, for which he has run the London Marathon. More frivolously, he often appears in lists of 'sexy men' on the planet.

Sadly for Essex, Dermot now lives in London, with his long-term Norwegian girlfriend, a producer.

Jamie Oliver, MBE

Chef

It is no surprise to find that Jamie was brought up in a pub-restaurant. His parents ran The Cricketers in the Essex village of Clavering and food was to be an important part of his life when he and his sister, Anne-Marie, were growing up.

He was born in 1975, and while still at primary school Jamie learned how to peel vegetables and help out in the kitchen, and he took an active interest in the family business. At Newport Free Comprehensive (now Grammar) in Saffron Walden, he preferred getting into scrapes to any form of academic study, and left with just one respectable exam pass – in Art.

Jamie Oliver. (Photograph by David Loftus)

As the most viable opportunity for the future, Jamie started a catering course at Westminster College when he was seventeen, his first work experience being in France. Although only there for three months, he realised that he was missing his childhood sweetheart, Juliette Norton. Upon his return, they were very much an item, planning a future with her as a model and him running a top restaurant. In the meantime, he worked as head pastry chef in the Neal Street Restaurant in London, followed by over three years at the River Café in Hammersmith.

While at River Café, a documentary was filmed (1996) and young Jamie stole the limelight to such an extent that a shrewd television producer eventually signed him up for the first series of *The Naked Chef*. His charisma, enthusiasm and infectious youth paved the way for future success, with cookbooks and further series.

In 2000, he and Jools were married at the thirteenth-century All Saints' Church in Rickling, near to where Jamie's parents were then living. He is even said to have got up at the crack of dawn to bake the bread for the wedding, and prepare his ideal wedding feast. Half the county's pub trade were invited, and the groom helicoptered in The Chemical Brothers from the Glastonbury Pop Festival. Instead of wedding presents, guests were asked to donate to The Stroke Association, both Jamie and Jools having lost close family members following strokes. After a three-week honeymoon in Italy, they settled in the new flat they had bought in Hampstead.

A year later Jamie was back on television with *Jamie's Kitchen*, hiring unemployed youngsters for his new East End restaurant, Fifteen. This too spawned a second series, and resulted in an MBE in the 2003 Honours listings. In the meantime, Jools had given birth to their first child, Poppy Honey, in March 2002. Daisy Boo followed in April 2003.

Jamie gradually became an international success with his cookbooks translated into twenty languages, selling millions of copies, and he established himself, even in the USA, as the first of a new breed of celebrity chefs. Add sales of cookware and the multi-million pound deal with Sainsbury's, and you can see how he has financed his Essex mansion, complete with outdoor pool. But there's more to Jamie Oliver than the trappings of fame: the Fifteen Foundation, helping disadvantaged youngsters, is now a global phenomenon, winning the Beacon Fellowship Prize for its founder.

Jamie's School Dinners moved Jamie's on-screen campaigning up a level, and prodded schools all over the country into taking action to provide healthier, more imaginative food for the nation's school-children. The series picked up a BAFTA award in 2007 for best factual series. *Jamie's Great Italian Escape* and, most recently, *Jamie at Home*, are just two more of the outlets for Jamie's talents, with international coverage and with sales of DVDs to match.

Incidentally, cooking and family are not the only loves of Jamie Oliver's life; there's also music. He has been part of a band called Scarlet Division since he was twelve and is a competent drummer. Few things would please him more than a hit record but his work schedule means that this is probably a step too far.

Ronnie O'Sullivan

Snooker Player

Ronnie's mum and dad met at Butlin's and married as teenagers. He was born in 1975 when they were living in the Birmingham area but they moved to Dalston, East London, as soon as a council flat came up, East London being his dad's home patch. Summer holidays, however, were spent with his mother's family – in Sicily. This explains Ronnie's middle name, Antonio.

They moved to Eton Road in Ilford, and Ronnie's sister Danielle was born in 1982. At this point, his mum stopped working, and dad became the main breadwinner – he had by now set up a chain of sex shops in Soho. He was doing well enough to enable a move to a bigger house in an upmarket area of Ilford: The Drive.

Ronnie O'Sullivan. (Author's Collection)

By the time Ronnie was seven, he was playing snooker on a small (6ft by 3ft) table at his uncle's house. His dad then joined a club at Green Lanes, Ilford, where Ronnie was allowed to play unofficially. At just nine Ronnie won his first (local) tournament and at ten, he became the youngest ever to make a century, making him a miniature snooker celebrity. Interestingly, he can play both right and left handed.

His schooling in Ilford was at Loxford Park – where he was bullied for being overweight – and at Highland School where, in contrast, he acquired a reputation as a bit of a hard man after knocking down George Palacaros, the school's tough guy (and later a personal friend). He was also, by then, earning as much as his teachers by travelling the country at weekends to play in tournaments. At home, his dad had built him a huge snooker room at the bottom of the garden, where he was able to practice for hours on end. This meant he won his first Pro-Am tournament at the age of fourteen, when the cue case was still bigger than he was.

At the English Amateur Festival in 1991, Ronnie became the youngest person in history to make the maximum 147 break, a record which still stands. Not surprisingly, he acquired a manager, Barry Hearn – but his first trip in a stretch limo with Barry was a visit to Brixton Prison where Ronnie O'Sullivan Senior had been locked up for an attack on Charlie Kray's driver. Ronnie's dad was sentenced to eighteen years, and obviously this had a profound effect on the whole family.

Family problems did not slow Ronnie up, however, and he went from number 800 in the world to 57 over the 1992/3 season. He won his first thirty-eight matches as a professional (a record) and his first title was the 1993 UK Championship, the youngest ever winner of a ranking tournament.

More family problems followed in 1994 when Ronnie's mum was sentenced to eighteen months in jail for tax evasion. Family friends looked after Danielle while the family home – now in Chigwell – was locked up and Ronnie travelled around. When Ronnie's mother was released, Ronnie left the family home, having antagonised his family with his drinking, his over-eating and his experiments with dope. A friendly chat with Graeme Souness, the footballer, put Ronnie on track to fitness, and to the fastest maximum in history in the 1997 World Championship – five minutes, twenty seconds. Hence his nickname: 'The Rocket'. Winning the World Championships inevitably followed: in 2001, 2004 and 2008.

Ronnie has invested in a substantial property portfolio (and even a lingerie shop in Soho) and lives near his parents' home in Chigwell. He has achieved a professional standard with his golf, and has become an advocate of running (he clocks up fifty miles a week) to stave off depression. Addiction, as Ronnie writes in his autobiography, is a big part of his life. On a good day, he's addicted to snooker. On a bad day it means checking into The Priory. He met his partner, Jo, through Narcotics Anonymous and they have two children Lily (born 2006) and Ronnie (2007). Having tried fishing, yoga, philosophy and religion, perhaps Ronnie O'Sullivan, popular and talented Essex boy, has found a way of dealing with his demons at last.

Tamzin Outhwaite

Actress

Ilford has been the source of many talented and celebrated individuals, and Tamzin Outhwaite is another for the Ilford list. Born in 1970, she and her two brothers grew up there, and Tamzin attended Trinity High School, a Catholic independent. Her family (Italian mum a financial advisor and dad a cab driver) still live in the area.

Tamzin Outhwaite. (Author's Collection)

'Showbiz' has always appealed to Tamzin, who went to the Stagestruck Theatre Co. from an early age, and later studied dance and drama at the London Studio Centre. She won an award for best all-rounder in her first year at the Centre. Not surprisingly, then, that less than a week after graduating, she was offered a part in a touring production of *Grease* – starting off in Swansea. Roles in *Men Behaving Badly* and *The Bill* soon came her way, although she has done other notable stage work, including serious dramas as well as musicals (*Oliver!* and *Carousel*).

Tamzin has been quoted as having 'loved' her upbringing, and having 'loved' growing up in Essex. However, some of her happiest times were earning a few hundred pounds a week touring when she was a teenager starting out.

Her biggest break came in 1998 when she was cast as Melanie Healy in *EastEnders*. The role meant that she was included in some high-profile story lines, marrying gangster Steve Owen for one (Martin Kemp's *alter ego*). This was the spring for her career, and Tamzin left the cast of *EastEnders* in 2002 to move on to plenty of additional television work – most notably in *Red Cap* and *Hotel Babylon*.

She has also been in a couple of films, but this side of her acting career has yet to take off in a big way, although she picked up a Variety award for her role in *Out Of Control*, which won the Edinburgh Festival award for best British film. 2007 saw her being acclaimed for her performance in *Boeing Boeing* at the Comedy Theatre in London. One of her biggest 'earners' has been the million pound contract to advertise Avon cosmetics, and presenting opportunities have also come her way. She has certainly managed to avoid the classic soap trap of being typecast.

Marriage to fellow 'EastEnder' – and nearly, but not quite, toy boy – Tom Ellis (who played Doctor Cousins) came in 2006 in a tiny island church on a lake at Orchardleigh House in Bath, her bridesmaid being the presenter Kate Thornton. The marriage followed a couple of abortive relationships with a deejay, a snowboarder, and another 'EastEnder'. The couple have settled in North London. Tamzin gave birth to her first baby in the summer of 2008.

Tony Parsons

Journalist and Writer

Born in 1953 in Romford, over his dad's shop, Tony Parsons grew up on a council estate. Vic Parsons (who was badly wounded during the Second World War) was a greengrocer, but later worked for a supermarket when the trade started struggling. At one time, he held down additional jobs as a lorry driver and a market stallholder so that his family could move out of their rented flat in Harold Hill to a semi-detached house in Billericay. Tony may have been an only child in a poor family, but luckily there was always money for books and time for reading with his literary and musical mum, Emma.

His school was the local grammar, which became comprehensive during his time there. He had already written a novel by the age of seventeen, but worked initially at Gordon's gin distillery in London until 1976 when his writing career began: as a (punk) music journalist on the *New Musical Express*. This was a pivotal year, when his first novel, *The Kids*, was published, and when he met fellow *NME* journalist Julie Burchill, marrying her a few years later. He has also written for the *Daily Telegraph*, and, more recently, the *Daily Mirror*.

Between 1976 and 1979 Tony lived in a bedsit in North London. During these years he led a somewhat wild life and became friends with many of the bands he wrote about. He describes this home as 'bohemian squalor, more squalor than bohemian'. He wrote a few more books after his *NME* experience, but returned to journalism in his thirties, writing for such magazines as *Elle* and *The Face*, while single-handedly bringing up his young son Bobby (Julie had left him in 1984).

Before finding widespread success as a mainstream novelist, Tony made guest appearances on some of the BBC's arts programmes including *The Late Review* – as the working class presence – and he wrote several books of cultural criticism.

He wrote *Man and Boy* after his father's death and his mother died of cancer shortly afterwards, so his beloved parents did not see the publishing phenomenon that *Man and Boy* became. Not only a bestseller on its 1999 publication, but a longseller which has now sold nearly two million copies in over twenty-five countries, with film rights sold for £1 million, and winning the coveted British Book of the Year award in 2001. Tony is, understandably, proud of the fact that this book reached people who don't normally buy books. His subsequent novels have all been best-sellers, focusing on popular lad-lit, although *Stories We Could Tell* harks back to the seventies and his days at the *NME*.

With such a track record, it is no surprise to find that he lives in a £2 million house in Hampstead. His second wife, Yuriko, is Japanese, and works as a translator. The couple have a daughter, Jasmine, who was born after they had been married for ten years, and she attends a private school in the area and goes to Japanese school on Saturdays.

Julia Roberts bought the screenplay of Tony's novel, *The Family Way*, although the project does not seem to have progressed. But Tony Parsons is not too depressed about it. His Japanese lessons are progressing, he has sold over four million books, he has a loving family and a BMW and – unlike his dad – he is not relying on winning the football pools on Saturday to finance a comfortable future.

Tony Parsons. (Courtesy of Karolina Webb)

Joe Pasquale

Comedian

Joe was born in 1961. Although he was born in the East End of London, he certainly did not stay there long, as he and his three siblings are always described as 'from Grays'. His dad worked in a margarine factory, and his mum was a housewife.

A pupil at Torrells Comprehensive School in Thurrock, he left school at fifteen, and embarked on a string of jobs – clerical work, factory jobs, a garage forecourt assistant, a plasterer, and what he describes as his worst job: welding at Ford's, Dagenham, during the night shift, which he managed for just two weeks. Once he began working at Warner Holidays as a Green Coat, however, he knew he had found his niche.

This was the start of Joe, the helium-voiced entertainer. Coming second in the grand final of *New Faces* in 1987 meant that he had finally arrived, doing what he did best, making people laugh. A number of years perfecting his stand up routine followed, and he competed again in 1993, this time winning the competition, and ending up at *The Royal Variety Show* (the first of five appearances there).

In the meantime, Joe had married, divorced and married for a second time (in 1986). His level of earnings in the '80s meant that he and his wife lived in a caravan – from 1984 to 1988 in Lowestoft - while he was still working mainly at holiday camps.

In the '90s, however, Joe went from strength to strength, featuring in his own television specials, recording many videos (his first had sales of over £1 million) and DVDs, touring with sell-out performances, and appearing in panto. In 1999, he took on an acting role in *The Nerd*, which was well received.

The one programme which really propelled Joe into the A list was his appearance in *I'm a Celebrity … Get me Out of Here!* in 2004, which he won after being the favourite from day one. Such a result triggered frequent requests for his presence in such programmes as *Saturday Night Takeaway* and *The Paul O'Grady Show*, and Joe's tours became ever more demanding and popular. He was especially pleased to have been the only British comedian to be asked to appear in the twenty-fifth anniversary of *The Muppet Show* in America in 2001, accompanying Jon Voight who became an instant fan.

Joe has also acquired a taste for acting in recent years, and has appeared in *Tom, Dick and Harry* (2003), *Rosencrantz and Guildenstern Are Dead* (2004), and most memorably in *The Producers* in London's West End (2007). His work on television has continued to expand, including numerous voice-overs and such shows as *The Price is Right* and *An Audience with Joe Pasquale*, the latter attracting an audience of nine million in 2005. But he hasn't left pantomime behind, breaking his own box office record as Buttons in the Cliffs Pavilion production of *Cinderella* in 2007/8 at Southend-on-Sea.

When he finally settled in a modest bungalow in Kent, Joe did not in fact spend very much time at home, as he was in such demand. But he found time to acquire a pilot's licence to offset the fear of flying he demonstrated in the Australian jungle in 2004, and he bought a telescope to follow another acquired interest, astronomy.

Sadly, Joe has split from Debbie, his wife of twenty years. He moved out of the family home and back in with his father, who had recently had a heart attack. Joe has three daughters from his first marriage, and two children from his second, aged between twelve and twenty-nine. But, although now a grandfather, he is a long, long way from retreating to his slippers and cocoa. In fact, it is not that long since he indulged in a rare extravagance – purchasing a Russian Yak aeroplane. Let's hope he doesn't fly too far from home.

Joe Pasquale. (Author's Collection)

Jim Peters

Athlete

Jim Peters, son of a railway clerk, was born in London in 1918, but moved to the Becontree Estate in Dagenham as a schoolboy. He took up running at the recommendation of the manager of Dagenham Boys' Club. It is reputed that he ran in slippers as he couldn't afford spikes, but still became champion of Essex over one mile before being called up for Army service in 1939.

Jim Peters. (Courtesy of Kingston AC & Polytechnic Harriers)

After starting his training as an optician on leaving Grafton School, he spent six years in the Royal Army Medical Corps near Southampton. During this period, he ground 75,000 pairs of respirator lenses 'soldiers for the use of'. Sport, however, continued to play a big part in his leisure time. His interest was not limited to athletics, because he considered becoming a soccer professional, having played with the legendary Alf Ramsey while in the Army. He went on to specialise in three- and six-mile runs and cross country, in spite of – or perhaps because of – his diminutive stature (5ft 6in).

Jim Peters is ironically remembered less for his bronze medal in the 1954 Empire Games 6-mile run than his failure in the marathon, when he collapsed, whilst seventeen minutes ahead of the rest of the field, just 85 yards from victory. Even worse, he had the additional humiliation of disqualification because he had been 'helped' off the track ... by supportive spectators who were, effectively, congratulating him. Subsequently, there have been suggestions that the course was in fact twenty-seven miles long, which would mean that he did cover the standard marathon distance.

The fear of collapsing like Peters is the reason that water stations are now provided along the route in most races of 10km and above today, bearing in mind that he was almost certainly dehydrated. Training for the marathon has certainly undergone many changes since Jim Peters' collapse, some small consolation perhaps.

He was captain of the England runners at the Vancouver Games (now the Commonwealth Games) following wins at home in the Polytechnic ('Poly') Marathon in four successive years (1951-1954). Each of these performances saw him beating his former British record time and establishing a world record of 2 hours 17 minutes in 1954. Apparently he broke at least one of these records wearing Woolworth's plimsolls!

International events were not so lucky for Peters. He retired (when in fourth position) from the Helsinki Olympics in 1952 with cramp. The 1954 Vancouver Marathon was staged in 86 degrees Fahrenheit in the shade, and

Peters and another English runner, Stan Cox, were affected. Even the entire Australian team dropped out.

Blood pressure problems led to Peters' retirement from athletics, but this enabled him to spend more time with his wife of fourteen years, Frieda. From 1954 onwards, he was also able to concentrate on his optical business, establishing three practices in and around London (one being at Chadwell Heath). However, he still ran as a V.I.P. guest in many marathons around the world.

Peters retired to Barnstaple Road, Thorpe Bay in 1979 to be nearer to his daughter Jennifer and the family. He became president of Dagenham Rotary Club, making guide dogs for the blind a fund-raising project. He also often acted as race starter in the 1990s for the Southend annual half-marathon, named after him, which still takes place. The Jim Peters Cup is presented to the first Essex-based finisher.

Although he died of cancer at Fair Havens Hospice in Westcliff-on-Sea in 1999, he will be remembered long after Joe McGhee, the real winner of that ill-fated 1954 marathon. He even received a 'special medal' at the instigation of the Duke of Edinburgh, inscribed: *J. Peters, a most gallant marathon runner.*

Ruth Pitter, CBE

Poet

Ruth's parents were both teachers in the East End of London. The family (including Ruth's two younger siblings) lived in Meath Road, Ilford, which is where she was born, in 1897. On her doorstep was Hainault Forest, which seems to have been a magical part of her childhood.

An early influence was the poetic taste of her parents, who encouraged family gatherings on Sunday to recite poems learned by heart. At some point, they had a cottage in even more rural surroundings at North End (South of Braintree), and the natural world was always the key to Ruth's burgeoning imagination.

The first poetry she had published was in *New Age*, when she was just fourteen. By this time, she was at Coborn School in East London. Ruth continued to write, and to be published, but she had to support herself and so worked for a small firm who made decorated furniture. She also spent a couple of years working for the War Office.

Ruth Pitter, by Robert Gardner. (Courtesy Enitharmon Press)

Hilaire Belloc had discovered her work through *New Age*, and financed the publication of her first collections in the 1920s and '30s. Even with such encouraging sponsorship, she found it necessary to start her own business with friend Kathleen O'Hara, again making decorative furniture and painted trays. She never married, but Eric Blair (George Orwell) and Lord David Cecil were among her friends.

Her 1934 work, *A Mad Lady's Garland*, reflecting her expertise in pastiche, attracted wider public attention, and she began to gather a following on both sides of the Atlantic. Her work was praised by Yeats and C.S. Lewis (the latter was particularly 'enamoured' of her 'metrical subtleties') and she received the Hawthornden Prize for *A Trophy of Arms* (1937) and the Heinemann Award for Literature with *The Ermine* (1954). She also received the Queen's Gold Medal for Poetry (1955) which was normally presented by the Poet Laureate, but, as Ruth was the first woman recipient, it was presented at Buckingham Palace by the Queen. Philip Larkin also included Ruth in his *Oxford Book of Modern Verse*.

After being bombed out in the Second World War, and working in a munitions factory, Ruth and Kathleen bought a house in rural Buckinghamshire with a garden, so Ruth could indulge another passion in her life. She maintained an extensive correspondence during this period with such luminaries as Siegfried Sassoon and Walter de la Mare.

Once she had established a literary reputation, she was invited on to radio and television programmes, one regular spot being on *The Brains Trust*. This offset her quiet home life where she continued her decorative painting into her seventies. From 1958 to 1959 she contributed weekly articles to *Woman* magazine on country living, gardening and religion.

In 1974, Ruth was made a Companion of Literature by the Royal Society of Literature, and five years later was awarded the CBE. Despite these honours, this Essex poet remains relatively unknown.

Blind by the end of her life, she died in 1992 and was buried in the churchyard of St Mary the Virgin near her final home in Long Crendon, Buckinghamshire.

With human bellow, bovine blare,
Glittering trumpery, gaudy ware,
The life of Romford market-square
Set all our pulses pounding …

from *Romford Market*

[Incidentally, her younger sister, Shirley Murrell, was a novelist in the 1940s and '50s – her books include *Young Man's Fancy* which featured Chigwell Row, *Gentlemen's Country* and *The Sin Flood* which featured other parts of Essex.]

Brian Poole

Pop Singer

Born in Barking in 1941, Brian's schooling was at the local Park Modern. His family made a living as butchers and market traders in London.

After seeing Buddy Holly perform live at East Ham Granada in 1958, Brian founded The Tremeloes, other members being friends with similar musical interests and ambitions. Alan Blakley and Alan Howard were from the same school, and Dave Munden was not far away, in Dagenham. They practised after school, and at one stage were even able to use a classroom to rehearse in.

Brian Poole. (Author's Collection)

Rather arbitrarily, Brian was chosen as the lead singer because the glasses he then wore resembled Buddy Holly's! The name 'Tremeloes' apparently came from the use of vibrato on the amplifier – otherwise known as tremolo. Graham Scott (also from Park Modern) joined them, and his dad took on management of the group, which started out playing mostly Buddy Holly numbers.

Brian and the others played at local cinemas in the intervals between films, and worked as studio-backing vocalists while their band built up a fan base performing at local U.S. airbases and dance halls. By 1960, the band, after a few changes to their line-up, had turned professional, and began a twenty-one week engagement at Butlin's in Ayr.

It was Essex fans (from Southend-on-Sea) who pestered BBC Radio to give the band a spot on *Saturday Club* with Brian Matthew, giving them much wider exposure. An audition with Decca followed (1962) resulting in their being signed up for a recording contract, an early hit being 'Twist and Shout', and their biggest No.1 being 'Do You Love Me?' During the early '60s, the band notched up eleven top ten hits, and their first major tour was with the then unknown Beatles – and they were the first band (and the last!) to appear on *Ready Steady Go*.

In Brian's career with The Tremeloes, Brian completed three world tours and numerous national tours, but the hits eventually dried up and Brian tried for a solo career in 1966. The Tremeloes continued to record successfully without him into the '70s, scoring a No.1 in their own right – 'Silence is Golden'. Brian concentrated for a while on his own record company, Outlook Records, as well as helping out in the family meat-packing business.

From the '70s onwards, he has been touring with new band Electrix, his *Reelin' 'n' Rockin' Show* receiving many accolades between 2001 and 2006. In 1986, Brian was pleased to be a part of the *Royal Variety Performance: A Royal Gala*. He has also worked in the UK and overseas with ex-members of such '60s bands as the Troggs, the Searchers, the Merseybeats, the Foundations and Gerry and the Pacemakers. In 2006, Brian Poole and the (original) Tremeloes re-formed for a national tour.

Interestingly, Brian's daughters (he has been married for well over thirty years) were successful band Alisha's Attic, although they now have separate careers in the music industry; and son-in-law Ally McErlaine is lead guitarist with contemporary band Texas. Music obviously runs through Brian's Essex veins.

Sir Alf Ramsey

Football Player and Manager

Alfred Ernest Ramsey was born in 1920 in Halbutt Street, Dagenham, near to where his father ran a smallholding (Five Elms Farm) in an area then surrounded by market gardens. He had three brothers, Cyril, Albert and Len. The boys had to walk a four-mile return journey to Becontree Heath School everyday. However, the tedium was relieved by incorporating the walk with kick-abouts along the way, so that all the boys learned ball control and the need for accurate passing to avoid the ditches.

At seven, Alf was picked for the school junior football team, but football was no more than a hobby when he left school to work for the local Co-op stores, delivering groceries on his bicycle. He had not managed to secure a job at the local Ford factory, but he was able to play football in his spare time for Five Elms United, a local team. He also spent some of his leisure at Dagenham Greyhound Stadium.

1940 was the date of his call-up to infantry training in Truro, the furthest he had been from home. He became quartermaster–sergeant in an anti-aircraft unit. His C.O. was a football fan, encouraging Alf, and when the battalion played Southampton in a friendly, the result was the offer of a place in their team in 1944 at the end of the war. When he was approached by Tottenham Hotspur in 1949, they were not the iconic team they are today, but Alf was attracted by the idea of being able to live at home in Dagenham. During his time at Tottenham, Alf married his girlfriend Vickie and they had a daughter.

He played at right-back in more than 250 cup and league games, and captained England three of the thirty-two times he played, acquiring the nickname 'The General'. His football career ended in 1955 following an injury, and he moved on to managing Ipswich Town. In seven years, he took them from Third Division strugglers to the League championship at their first attempt in 1961-1962. His Ipswich team had been put together for just £30,000!

Such success meant that he was appointed England manager in 1963, but he stayed living in Ipswich, having made the town his home. As everyone in England knows, Alf Ramsey went on to lead the England team to victory in the 1966 World Cup. He achieved what no one else has done before or since, with the help, incidentally, of two other Essex footballers: Bobby Moore and Geoff Hurst.

However, following the next two World Cups, losing to Germany in the quarter-final in 1970, and failing to qualify in 1974, the writing was on the wall. Later that season, Alf Ramsey, the man who had received a knighthood for his services to football (1967), was sacked.

After eighteen months out of football Alf joined the board of Birmingham City, and did well as caretaker manager between September 1977 and March 1978. Poor health precipitated early retirement, but Alf Ramsey continued to visit Wembley for every major footballing occasion.

During the world cup finals in 1998, Alf suffered a stroke, and he died at a nursing home in Ipswich in 1999. His name and reputation live on, and he entered the Football Association Hall of Fame in 2002.

Alf Ramsey. (Courtesy of 'TURF' Cigarettes)

Ruth Rendell, CBE

Writer

Ruth Rendell was born in 1930, but her earliest childhood, like many of her books, is shrouded in mystery. She doesn't discuss it in interviews, though it seems that her earliest years were spent in either Woodford or in Leyton (East London) before moving to Shelley Grove, Loughton and attending Loughton County High School for Girls. Her parents were teachers in East London, her mother coming to the UK as a child after spending her own formative years in Sweden and Denmark. The family spent holidays in Scandinavia and Ruth learned both Swedish and Danish.

After giving birth to Ruth, Ebba Graseman (or Grassmann) developed multiple sclerosis, and it is interesting that, utilising the pseudonym of Barbara Vine, Ruth Rendell has written about the effects of long-term illness in family generations.

When Ruth left school at eighteen, she worked as a reporter and sub-editor on the *Chigwell Times* where she met her husband Ron Rendell. They married when she was twenty, and had a son, Simon, in 1953. At some stage it seems she was actually fired from her job as a journalist when she wrote up the annual dinner for a local Essex tennis club, although she had not attended it and had thus missed the death of the after dinner speaker in mid-speech. This incident surely had the makings of a great start for another novel.

For nearly a decade, Ruth stayed at home as a housewife, spending her free time writing stories in various genres until hitting on success in 1964 with her first crime novel, *From Doon with Death*, debuting Detective Inspector Reginald Wexford. Her reputation grew with every book, and some of her fiction is set in Epping Forest. There is a hilly area of Loughton close to the Forest which she describes as Little Cornwall in *The Face of Trespass*, and which has since adopted this name.

Since that first Wexford novel, Ruth has written thirty-eight Rendell novels and eleven Vines as well as collections of short stories. Her books have been translated into twenty-five languages, as well as being televised, and the Queen of Crime has won many awards including the coveted diamond, gold and silver daggers from the Crime Writers' Association and Edgars from the Mystery Writers of America. Her phenomenal global success has made her a millionaire several times over. As much as £100,000 per annum of her earnings is donated to charities, including the Royal National Institute for the Blind.

She divorced Don in 1975 but re-married him two years later, and, until his death in 1999, they lived in a sixteenth-century farmhouse in a remote location near Polstead in Suffolk. He lived to see his wife honoured with a CBE in 1996 and created a life peer by the Labour Government in 1997.

Baroness Rendell of Babergh (Suffolk) writes in the mornings and attends the House of Lords in the afternoon. She has a London base in Maida Vale, and her son lives in Colorado with his family. Arguably, Ruth Rendell is the most successful female writer Essex has produced.

Ruth Rendell. (Author's Collection)

Sade, OBE

Singer-Songwriter

Helen Folesade Adu was born in Nigeria in 1959 but moved to Colchester when she was just four, following the separation of her parents. Her mother, Anne Hayes, was an English nurse, and her father was a Nigerian professor of economics.

Her first school was Heathlands Primary in West Bergholt, but it seems that when her mother re-married (in 1970), the family moved to Clacton-on-Sea, and Helen then attended Clacton County High School. As a teenager, Helen worked in several part-time jobs, including waitressing and as a bike messenger. Free time, however, was devoted to her favourite music – Billie Holiday, Nina Simone, Marvin Gaye and Al Green.

On leaving school, she studied art and design at the Colchester Institute before progressing to a three-year course in fashion design at St Martin's School of Art in London, while continuing to work part-time as a model. On graduating, she set up a small fashion company making men's clothes with her friend, Gioia, who went on to designing some of Helen's stage costumes in later years.

Music was still an interest, however, and she was able to indulge her taste for soul music at American Air Force bases in Ilford and Canvey Island. Another part-time pursuit was as a singer, and she began to treat her music more seriously after joining a Latin funk collective called Pride. With fellow Pride members, this evolved by early 1984 into her own group, with Sade (as she was now known) as lead singer and songwriter securing a contract with Epic Records.

Sade's 1984 single 'Smooth Operator', which reached platinum sales, is still her best known work, and was included in her 2005 album *Best of Sade*. Her debut album, *Diamond Life*, reached the top ten, and also went platinum in 1985 when it reached the U.S. top five. Her first Grammy Award followed – for best new artist – and the sales of *Diamond Life* also meant that she was awarded a Brit for Best Album, and went on to appear in the Live Aid Concert.

Further hits followed for the band, and Sade appeared in the film *Absolute Beginners*, but subsequently moved to Madrid for a while to escape the tide of public interest. Here she married – and subsequently divorced – the Spanish film-maker Carlos Scola. (Her mother, incidentally, stayed in Clacton and became a sister at Clacton Maternity Hospital.)

When the band re-convened, further successes followed. The album *Love Deluxe* in 1992 spent ninety weeks on the Billboard chart, and has two additional claims to fame: it featured Sade topless and painted gold on its cover, and one track ('No Ordinary Love', later a successful single) accompanied the controversial Robert Redford film of 1993, *Indecent Proposal*. 'No Ordinary Love' resulted in a second Grammy for Best Rhythm and Blues Performance.

In 1996, Sade's daughter Isla Morgan was born, but she was still singing, touring and recording. When she finally released new material with *Lovers Rock* in 2000, it sold three million copies in America alone, and made her the biggest selling UK act that year. Her 2001 Grammy followed a sell out American tour, and was for Best Pop Vocal Album.

Sade was the eleventh highest female earner in the UK in 2001, and did even better in 2005, reaching number six, above the Spice Girls. Her biggest accolade was the OBE presented to her at Buckingham Palace in 2002 for services to popular music. This award she regarded as a great gesture not only to her, but for 'all black women in England'. A remarkable come-back for a remarkable Essex girl, who has sold well over forty million albums worldwide.

Sade. (Author's Collection)

Sandie Shaw

Pop Singer

Sandra Goodrich was born in 1947 in Dagenham into one of the many families who had moved from East London to the Dagenham estates after the war. As both her parents worked, she stayed after school with 'Aunt' Daph and her two daughters. They lived over the road, and Sandie recalls, in her autobiography, how this neighbour used to re-plait her long hair – not a pleasant experience. She was an only child, destined for a job at the local Ford factory.

Sandie showed an early interest in singing, starting with the Irish social clubs her parents visited on Friday nights, and from the age of twelve she started going to local dance halls. She was regularly invited up on stage to sing, and managed a respectable second place in a singing contest at the Ilford Palais when she was sixteen. On Sundays she attended all the services at the local Baptist church with one girlfriend, and moved on to a Catholic mass with another so she could join in all the singing. School days were at Robert Clack Grammar School, Dagenham.

It was Ford's that presented her with her first pay cheque, for £7 15s 11d. However, she admits to not really earning this, preferring to find reasons to spend time in the sick bay or to draw caricatures on the cards she was supposed to punch holes in.

Following an appearance on stage at Hammersmith in 1963 she met Adam Faith, who introduced her to his agent, Eve Taylor. That saw an end to the Ford's pay cheques. Sandie had her first No. 1 single at just seventeen with 'Always Something There to Remind Me'.

Her coming-of-age cheque from her agent could have bought her a town house in Knightsbridge and a country estate, but she settled for putting a deposit on a house in Blackheath, because her new husband wanted to pay his own way and share the repayments. Sandie had married fashion designer Jeff Banks in 1968, having met him in her agent's office over a year earlier. They seemed the perfect '60s partnership of fashion and pop and Sandie got involved in Jeff's business ventures.

Sandie's win in the Eurovision Song Contest in 1967 – the first Brit to do this – was the most conclusive win in its history. 'Puppet on a String' went on to be a huge hit, and by the end of the '60s she had notched up over twenty Top Forty hits, including more number ones than any other female British artist.

Her daughter Grace was born in 1971, but Jeff's business went under in the '70s slump and the family ended up penniless. This was a dark decade for Sandie, who tried her hand at songwriting and different ventures to enable her to spend time with Grace – songwriting, theatre (Ophelia in *Hamlet*, Joan of Arc in *St Joan*), painting – and started her lifelong commitment to Buddhism. In the end, it was primarily Jeff's concentration on his business interests that drove the couple apart, and Sandie Shaw succumbed to Nik Powell's determined wooing in 1981, after she had been separated from Jeff for three years.

Her marriage to Nik, the co-founder of the Virgin Group, lasted fifteen years. They had two children, Amie (who became a model) and Jack.

Sandie made her first pop video in 1982 for the single 'Anyone Who Had a Heart' and re-started a recording career in 1984 with The Smiths. But the showbiz world was beginning to pall a little and she studied psychotherapy for three years, qualifying as a counsellor in 1994. Over the years she has taught and introduced hundreds of people to Buddhism, and this interest she shares with Tony Bedford, who became her third husband in 1996 after an amicable divorce from Nik.

First British recording star to perform behind the Iron Curtain, first female artist to produce and own her masters and copyright ... this is one iconic Essex girl who will stay in the record books.

Sandie Shaw. (Author's Collection)

Ben Shephard

Television Presenter

A familiar television face these days, Ben was born in 1974 and went to Chigwell School (Independent). A sporting boy at school, he was an accomplished rugby and football player, and of course has been seen much more recently beating off Lemar at a Sport Relief boxing match, demonstrating his ongoing fitness. While at school, he played for both the South East England's Under 16 and Under 18 football teams, and for the Senior Eastern Counties rugby team.

Ben Shephard (with Claire Sweeney). (Author's Collection)

At eighteen he chose Birmingham University to study dance, drama and theatre arts, and achieved a 2:1 BA Honours. He has also achieved fluency in French, useful when he worked for a while in a French wine chateau. It was at Birmingham University that he met his future wife, Annie, who apparently enjoyed watching him dance.

It wasn't until 1998 that Ben actually first appeared on television – presenting *Control Freaks* on Channel 4 (a teen programme) – up until then he had been working for production companies, waiting for his break. This first opportunity was the result of an interview for another children's show (*Diggit*) – he didn't get the job, but met Andi Peters who employed him for *T4*. Higher and higher profile shows followed: *Bedrock*, *The Bigger Breakfast*, *The Xtra Factor*, *Entertainment Today*, *Dance X*, the National Lottery's *1 vs 100*, and, perhaps most successfully, as long term co-presenter on *GMTV Today*.

Although primarily employed by ITV, Ben has also hosted his own radio show for London's Magic Radio on Saturday mornings. He has worked for the BBC on such projects as *EastEnders Revealed* and for MTV, Heat Radio, Channel 5 and Sky One. Most recently, he has been seen on *Britain's Got More Talent* on ITV2 and with Essex girl Denise Van Outen in 2008 in ITV's *Who Dares Sings*.

Having married Annie in 2004, they and their sons Samuel (born May 2005) and Jack (born January 2007) live in South West London, nearer to Ben's working base. He remains a fervent West Ham supporter, however, although more recent sporting interests include wakeboarding, kite-surfing and racing Fiestas for Team Ford.

Ben also returns to his Chigwell roots for such events as the Haven House Moulin Rouge Ball fund-raiser which was held at the Metropolitan Police Sports Ground in 2007.

On an undomestic note, in 2007 he was voted (by Ann Summers customers) the man most women would like to sleep with on St George's Day, beating Daniel Craig and Orlando Bloom. Another accolade for Essex perhaps?

Joan Sims

Actress

Irene Joan Marion Sims, an only child, was born in 1930 in the station house at Laindon where her father was the station master. Her early education was at St John's school in Billericay and the plaque on the Laindon house records her presence there from birth until 1952, the year she made her London stage debut.

Long before then, however, Joan was entertaining the Laindon station commuters. They seemed to have enjoyed her exuberant dancing and singing while they waited for trains. She has written of an absence of affection in childhood, driving her motivation to please, and she loved dressing up.

Her ties with Essex are irrefutable. Her mother was from Great Wakering, her father from Grays, her grandfather from Barling. Summer holidays were spent with her aunt Florence – 'Floss' – at Orchard House in Great Wakering when the area was very rural. Her uncle ran a successful fruit business there. In fact, she was staying at Orchard House in September 1939 when she heard Chamberlain's radio announcement that Britain was at war with Germany.

Her first taste of playing to audiences was in her teens with a local amateur dramatic society, the Langdon Players. At the South East Essex Drama Festival in 1946, she won her first award, for Best Individual Performance. It took her four auditions, however, to get into RADA and only then after a lengthy stint at PARADA (RADA's prep school in North London). One of Joan's holiday jobs while at RADA was as assistant stage manager at the repertory theatre that then existed at Southchurch, in Southend. Appearing on stage during her employment there was Stratford Johns, later famous as *Z Cars'* Chief Inspector Barlow.

On graduation, she secured an agent and began to work steadily (including being the voice of a BBC television puppet!) and her first film was *Colonel March Investigates* in 1952. In 1953, her role in *Will Any Gentleman* paid £25. However, another 1953 role, as Nurse Rigor Mortis in *Doctor in the House* saw her film career take off.

The offer of a role in *Carry on Nurse* did not strike Joan as significant, although the earlier *Carry on Sergeant* had been a box office success. However, it became number one at the British box office in 1959, and her earliest fame and popularity were almost certainly mainly attributable to the characters she played in the *Carry On* (twenty-four of them, achieving the greatest unbroken run of *Carry On* performances) and *Doctor* films. One of her own favourites, however, was the 1975 *Love Among the Ruins*, because of the opportunity to work with the legendary Laurence Olivier, Katharine Hepburn and director George Cukor.

Joan's explanation for the fact that she never married, in spite of several proposals (including one from Kenneth Williams!), is simply that she did not meet the right man. Male companions included – briefly – the glamorous Tyrone Power.

By the 1980s, Joan had lost many of her close friends and family, including her parents, Hattie Jacques, and her agent. Drink now became Joan's friend, as she freely admitted. The tabloids gave her a hard time during this period, but even a minor breakdown did not stop offers coming in, from a harrowing television role as child murderer Amelia Dyer to Fairy Sweetcorn in panto at the Richmond Theatre.

Television work saw Joan re-invented in her later years. *As Time Goes By* and *On the Up* gave her memorable roles, and the latter produced her only catch phrase: 'Just the one'. Betsy Prig in *Martin Chuzzlewit* was one of many remarkable roles that established her as a character actress, with an extraordinary range. In spite of health problems, Joan continued to work until shortly before her death in 2001. Her epitaph is summed up in her autobiography: 'Tyrone Power cut the rind off my bacon. They can't take that away from me.'

A plaque commemorating the actress Joan Sims. (Photograph by Dee Gordon)

Anne Stallybrass

Actress

Born in 1938 and raised in Westcliff-on-Sea, Anne was educated at St Bernard's Convent School in Milton Road, a school known for promoting its drama curriculum. Her parents were keen on amateur dramatics, and Anne was roped in – as the only child – in performances of such gems as Winnie-the-Pooh in the living room.

After school, she spent three years at the Royal Academy of Music, winning the Drama Gold Medal. Anne joined the Arthur Brough Players in Folkestone (Kent) as an assistant stage manager, finishing up eighteen months later as a leading lady. At Folkestone, interestingly, they performed tea matinées, seats being replaced by rows of tables with tea served in the interval, the only theatre in England doing this. While with the Arthur Brough Players, Anne returned several times to Westcliff-on-Sea, appearing in five different productions at the Palace Theatre in the '60s.

Next, Anne joined the Nottingham Playhouse and then worked in Sheffield, where she married her first husband, Roger Rowland, in 1963. The newlyweds moved to London, where Anne secured her first television roles – in such '60s productions as *Emergency Ward 10*. A few years later, she landed a starring role as Jane Seymour opposite Keith Michell in *The Six Wives of Henry VIII*, the part that was really her big break (1970).

As Anne Onedin in *The Onedin Line* (1971), Anne became a household name, and the series ran successfully over a number of years. During the '70s, Anne continued her work in theatre, touring with John Inman, for instance, in *My Fat Friend,* and with Eric Sykes in *Time and Time Again.* This was her decade, because she also appeared on television as *The Mayor of Casterbridge*'s wife, co-starring with Alan Bates, and as Anna Strauss in *The Strauss Family* for which she received the 1972 *TV Times* Best Actress Award. Apart from costume dramas, she was in demand for other television productions such as *Softly, Softly* (an early police series). Her speciality during this period (again, with several appearances at The Palace Theatre, Westcliff-on-Sea) seemed to be long-suffering wives.

In 1972, Anne and her first husband separated, and, by the end of the '70s, she had set up home with her *Onedin* co-star, Peter Gilmore. This led to a lot of unwanted publicity for the couple, who eventually married in 1987 after living together for ten years. The ceremony was a quiet civil union in Richmond, and the Gilmores have since spent most of their time in Dartmouth, their home nostalgically close to the setting of the *Onedin* filming location (it was disguised as the 1860 version of Liverpool). They have a London base in Barnes, and both homes have a garden to gratify Anne's horticultural interest and talent.

Both Anne and Peter have continued their acting careers, easing up as they reached state retirement age, which is not the same as acting-retirement-age.

For Anne, the 1980s resulted in another very successful television series (for Yorkshire Television): *Flying Lady*, plus other television one-offs (including Agatha Christie novels) and plenty of theatre. In the '90s, she turned up in such popular programmes as *Casualty* and *Midsomer Murders*, and was cast as the Queen in *Diana: Her True Story* in 1993. More recently she has been busy with radio work as well as playing roles in *Where The Heart Is*, *Murder in Mind*, etc.

We may not see much of her in Essex these days, but Anne Stallybrass has entertained us for more years than she may care to remember.

Anne Stallybrass. (Author's Collection)

Jack Straw

Politician

A famous name, a famous face in politics, and up-front about his Essex roots, Jack was born John Straw in Buckhurst Hill, in 1946. His Essex-born mother Joan was a teacher and his father Walter an insurance salesman. They divorced when he was ten, and he and his four siblings were brought up by his single mother in a council maisonette on a Loughton estate.

He attended Staples Road County Primary, followed by Brentwood School as a scholarship pupil. There has been speculation that he was not only bullied, but a bully, when at Brentwood School. Whatever the truth, it is a fact that Jack came from some radical roots – his mother was an Islington councillor in later life, and his grandfather was a shop steward. By the age of twelve, Jack was on his way to a political career – he was an Aldermaston marcher that year, and the following year he made an election speech at the local Labour meeting.

By the age of fourteen, he had achieved a remarkable ten O-levels, and was made deputy head boy. He adopted the name of Jack in honour of the Peasant Revolt leader. At Leeds University, he achieved a, for him, disappointing 2:2 for his law degree as a result of the time he had put into student union activism. As president of the National Union of Students, he had built the NUS into a powerful bargaining tool.

Nevertheless, he turned down political offers at this stage, and returned to his bar finals, coming third in the country. He practised for a while as a criminal law junior but kept up his political interests by sitting as an Islington councillor (until 1978), becoming deputy leader of the ILEA at age twenty-six, and standing as Labour parliamentary candidate in the 1974 election in Tonbridge, a Tory stronghold.

Realising then that his heart was more in politics than law, he accepted an offer to be special adviser to Labour MP Barbara Castle, a knowledgeable and influential mentor.

In the meantime, Jack had married Anthea Weston (in 1968). Their daughter was born in 1976, but sadly dying from a heart defect after just a few days, and shortly afterwards their marriage broke up. A year later, he quit politics for a while to work as a researcher on *World in Action*, but couldn't turn down the chance of Castle's Blackburn seat which she offered to him when she stood down.

He met his second wife, Alice, in Whitehall when she was a director at the Department of Health. They honeymooned in India in 1978, giving Jack an insight into the huge Asian population that made up his Blackburn constituency. Alice's inherited cottage in Oxfordshire is where they escape at weekends with children William and Charlotte.

After over a decade of loyal service to the party, it is no surprise that he managed Tony Blair's leadership campaign in the '90s. Nor is it unexpected

Jack Straw. (Author's Collection)

that he should have been offered the Home Secretary's job in 1997. In Gordon Brown's cabinet, he has been elevated to Justice Secretary and Lord Chancellor.

Adam Patel, a Blackburn friend, has said of Jack that he has made 'more progress on the race issue than anyone ever before' and it is an issue which remains close to his heart. As an asthmatic, as someone who has overcome a hearing loss in later life, and with his council-estate roots, Jack has overcome many obstacles to achieve the sort of success that can actually make a difference.

Dick Turpin

Highwayman

Baptised in Hempstead in September 1705, Richard Turpin was one of several sons born to John and Mary Turpin. John was a butcher by trade, but was also latterly the owner of the Blue Bell Inn at Hempstead.

It is not easy to separate fact from legend where Dick Turpin is concerned. Certainly he kept a low profile during his early life, and, although he was married, parish records of the union do not survive. Even the name of his wife varies – Elizabeth or Hester were the most often quoted, and her most likely occupation was that of maidservant. Of the early careers attributed to Dick Turpin, certainly he seems to have followed in his father's footsteps as a butcher, but whether this was Whitechapel in East London or at Thaxted is difficult to confirm – perhaps both.

'Dick Turpin' (Fictionalised image by T. Walter West, *The Graphic*, December 1900)

His criminal activities may have begun with stealing cattle which he could butcher and sell, but he was also likely to have been involved with poaching and smuggling activities in Essex. It is the poaching that would have brought him into contact with the notorious Essex Gang who seem to have started out stealing deer belonging to King George II from the Royal Forest of Waltham, stealing that became a serious problem for the verderers (forest officials) from 1730 onwards. The Gregory Brothers, who led the Gang, were gun-wielding career criminals with a taste for house-breaking. There are many reports of their robbing residences in and around Woodford, Chingford, Barking, Epping, Great Parndon and Loughton, although they seemed to have made the occasional foray into Kent and Surrey.

By the time Dick Turpin can be identified as a member of the gang, the robberies included gratuitous violence and even rape at gunpoint. The *London Gazette* in February 1735 described members of the Essex Gang who had not been apprehended, and the description of Richard Turpin is, with hindsight, perhaps a little disappointing: 'a tall fresh-coloured man, very much marked with the small pox ... about five feet nine inches high ... wears a blue grey coat and a natural wig'. [Notice 'tall' in 1735 was 5ft 9in.]

By now, Turpin had added highway robbery to his accomplishments, as had other gang members. It was in a cave in Epping Forest close to High Beech, one of several hiding places, that he added murder to his growing list of crimes when Thomas Morris (who worked for one of the forest keepers) attempted to capture him, but was shot and killed on attempting to do so. [The cave, incidentally, can still be seen.]

Interestingly, *Reid's Weekly Journal* of 14 May 1737 commented that 'The people about Epping Forest say he (Dick) will never be taken till a proclamation is published offering a reward'. This was exactly what happened, with a proclamation issued on 25 June offering £200 for his discovery, and adding to his description a reference to his 'broad' cheekbones, 'upright' stance and 'broad' shoulders. By then, Turpin, the most wanted criminal in England, was heading north.

Sadly, however, there is no evidence of any kind of hotly-pursued romantic flight to York, nor of Black Bess, his faithful steed. This journey and this horse appear in a fictionalised account of Turpin's life published in 1834: *Rookwood* by William Harrison Ainsworth. However, these elements of the Dick Turpin story live on, and are an integral part of the twenty-first-century legend.

More prosaically, Dick Turpin, calling himself John Palmer, went into hiding, but did not change his lifestyle, and was arrested for horse-stealing in October 1738. Eventually identified as the wanted Richard Turpin, his execution took place in April 1739. His fame lingers on world-wide, although his Essex roots are not as universally known perhaps.

Denise Van Outen

Television Presenter and Actress

The world of showbiz was always going to be the destiny of this Essex girl. At just seven years old she was already putting on shows for the neighbours and modelling knitting patterns for the sort of cash that her East End mother (a child carer) and Tilbury-docker turned security-guard father could only wonder at.

The family came from council-house roots, with Denise, the youngest of three, starting life in Basildon Hospital in 1974. They moved early on to Stanford-le-Hope where Denise attended St Joseph's Roman Catholic Primary School, and she was also a student at Susan Stephen's Theatre School in Corringham.

Before she made the jump to the prestigious Sylvia Young Theatre School in Marylebone, London, Denise had appeared on a West End stage – at the age of nine – in the cast of *Les Miserables*. While at Sylvia Young's she had to be on the 6 a.m. coach from Basildon to London every day, and the school fees were paid with her income from modelling and television commercials.

As a teenager, Denise had a few brief television roles, starting out as Denise Douglas. She became Denise Van Outen because it sounded more interesting (although whether there are any Dutch roots is debatable, her real name being plain Outen). She also did some professional singing engagements, mainly backing vocals. For a while she earned extra cash as a glamour model, but by the age of twenty-one she had got herself noticed for different reasons: as the attractive and cheeky weather and travel reporter on *The Big Breakfast*. She soon joined Johnny Vaughan as a popular co-presenter, and the duo became quite a hit towards the end of the '90s.

After a mistaken choice of exposure in *Something for the Weekend* on Channel 4, with some '90s television crumbs in *The Bill* and in the sit-com *Babes in The Wood*, Denise reinvented herself when her musical career took off with her debut as Roxie in *Chicago* in 2001. Two years later, she starred in *Tell Me On A Sunday*, her first one-woman show which toured the UK in 2004.

Since then, Denise has gone global. Having successfully played Roxie on Broadway, she has pursued work in America, featuring on the panel for such reality shows as *Any Dream Will Do* (reprising her UK position) and has even been a judge for *Miss World* in Poland.

More recently, Denise has appeared in *Rent* in London's West End, has been on television judging *I'd Do Anything*, and has resumed her professional relationship with Johnny Vaughan but on Capital Radio this time. The end of 2007 also saw her appearing in *The Empress's New Clothes*, part of a BBC series of revamped fairytales, when viewers had a chance to see that famous (in 1999) Rear of the Year. In 2008, Denise featured in *Who Dares Sings* with fellow Essex presenter, Ben Shephard.

Her career has been more successful than, perhaps, her personal life, which has featured in the tabloids over the years – a broken engagement to Essex boy Jay Kay of Jamiroquai, and other failed relationships with high-profile celebrities including Gary Glitter. However, Denise's parents have a long and successful marriage and Denise is hoping to repeat their experience in the not too distant future. In the meantime, she is building a secure property portfolio to offer a different kind of security. She may be blonde, but she's no bimbo.

Denise Van Outen. (Author's Collection)

Michael Wilding

Actor

Some of the most beautiful women in the world fell in love with Michael Wilding. That probably says it all.

This popular 1940s film star was born in Leigh-on-Sea in July 1912. His parents had been living in South West London but, after three years of childless marriage, had been advised by the family doctor to move to the seaside! Leigh-on-Sea was the choice, near enough to London to enable his father to travel to his job in the Russian Diplomatic Corps (he was born in Petrograd).

Brother Alistair came along in 1910 and Michael followed when his mother, a Scottish actress, was forty-two years old. His doting parents sent him to Christ's Hospital School, which then charged 'a sum according to one's means' and he showed a flair for art, resulting in a year studying in Bruges. Upon his return, when trying to get work in 1933 as a designer at Elstree, it was suggested to him that, because of his height (6ft 1in) he could stand in for Douglas Fairbanks Junior. *Catherine the Great*, released in 1934, was thus his introduction to acting.

Gradually, Michael climbed his way up the cast list, his career really taking off when he was cast as Anna Neagle's leading man in *Piccadilly Incident* in 1946. The duo's series of romantic comedies were extremely popular with cinema-goers keen to escape the deprivation of austerity and rationing of post-war Britain.

His first marriage was to Kay Young in 1938, a Joan Crawford look-alike he met when they were in the same revue at the Gate Theatre. The marriage did survive the war, but not for long. An obsession with Marlene Dietrich which started when they were filming Alfred Hitchcock's *Stage Fright* in 1950 didn't help matters, and being separated once Michael was filming in Hollywood a year later sealed their marital fate.

By the time their marriage was dissolved in 1952, Michael had met Elizabeth Taylor in Hollywood and been completely bowled over, although she was only twenty at the time, exactly half his age. Liz wasted little time in ousting Marlene and proposing marriage after her divorce from Nick Hilton. The marriage produced two sons, but, predictably perhaps, floundered in the wake of the age and temperamental differences, and the divergent career paths – his going down, hers up. They parted company in 1957 and Liz married Mike Todd.

Michael's remaining months in Hollywood were forgettable. Fired in the end for fluffing his lines on set (following one of the blackouts he had experienced for years) he returned to Britain. It was now 1958 and Michael Wilding was no longer a top box office name in his home country. He tried life as an agent, and was persuaded to marry rich businesswoman Susan Nell during this period. This proved to be a mistake on both their parts, and the marriage was quickly dissolved.

Undeterred, but finally giving such a momentous decision a little more thought, he met and married Margaret Leighton (1964) and also made a bit of a come-back in supporting roles in popular films at the end of the 1960s, e.g. *Waterloo* and *Lady Caroline Lamb*. Although Michael's star was still fading, this time Michael felt that Margaret's rising star was not a problem. Sadly for him, the wife he'd hoped to grow old with developed multiple sclerosis, playing her last few roles in a wheelchair.

Margaret died in 1976, aged fifty-three, and Michael was finally diagnosed with epilepsy in 1977, which explained his frequent blackouts. In 1979, he died after a particularly nasty fall following another seizure. Liz Taylor flew in for his funeral, and the *Daily Telegraph* announced his death as 'Gentleman Actor Dies' – Michael would have liked that.

Michael Wilding. (Author's Collection)

Select Bibliography

Bailey, Jack *Trevor Bailey, A Life in Cricket* (Methuen; London, 1993)

Ball, Kenny *Blowing my own Trumpet* (John Blake Publishing; London, 2004)

Bloom, Ursula *No Lady Meets No Gentleman* (Sampson, Low, Marston & Co.; London, 1940)

Bowler, Dave *Winning Isn't Everything* (Orion Books Ltd; London, 1999) (Alf Ramsey)

Brand, Russell *My Booky Wook* (Hodder & Stoughton; London, 2007)

Collins, Andrew *Still Suitable For Miners - Billy Bragg* (Virgin Books Ltd; London, 2002)

Couzyn, Jeni (Ed.) *The Bloodaxe Book of Contemporary Women Poets* (Bloodaxe Books; Newcastle-upon-Tyne, 1985) (Denise Levertov)

Greaves, Jimmy *Greavsie, The Autobiography* (Time Warner Books; London, 2003)

Gunnell, Sally & Christopher Priest *Running Tall* (Bloomsbury Publishing; London, 1995)

Hall, Donald (Ed.) *Contemporary American Poetry* (Penguin; USA, 1962)

Harman, James *Secrets, Loves and Lip Gloss* (Best Books Online, 2005) (Kathy Kirby)

Hildred, Stafford and Tim Ewbank *Jamie Oliver* (Blake Publishing; London, 2002)

Holloway, Sara (Ed.) *Family Wanted, True Stories of Adoption* (Granta Books; London, 2005) (Bernard Cornwell)

Holm, Ian *Acting My Life* (Bantam Press; London, 2004)

Madeley, Richard and Judy Finnigan *Richard and Judy, The Autobiography* (Coronet Books; London, 2002)

Moorehead, Caroline *Sidney Bernstein* (Jonathan Cape Ltd; London, 1984)

O'Sullivan, Ronnie (with Simon Hattenstone) *Ronnie, The Autobiography* (Orion Books Ltd; London, 2004)

Oxford Dictionary of National Biography (Oxford University Press, 2004-8)

Paskin, Barbara *Dudley Moore* (Sidgwick and Jackson; London, 1997)

Shaw, Sandie *The World at My Feet* (Harper Collins Publishers; London, 1991)

Simpson, M.J. *Hitchhiker, A Biography of Douglas Adams* (Coronet Books; London, 2003)

Sims, Joan *High Spirits* (Corgi Books; London, 2001)

Thatcher, Carol with Chris and John Lloyd *Lloyd on Lloyd* (Willow Books; London, 1985)

Wilding, Michael *Apple Sauce* (George Allen & Unwin; London, 1982)